HOW TO SING

The complete guide to singing, performing and recording

CARRIE & DAVID GRANT

CARLTON

CD Exercises - at a glance

START WITH YOUR BREATHING EXERCISE
With the CD

1. HUMMING

2. SPEAK-SINGING

(i)   'I am learning how to sing'
       'I am learning how to sing'
(ii)   'That is why I am practising'
       'That is what I am practising'
(iii) 'I am learning as I go'
       'I am learning as I go'
(iv)   'Learning fast and learning slow'
       'Learning fast and learning slow'
(v)   'I'm developing my range'
       'I'm developing my range'
(vi)   'Soon I'll start to hear a change'
       'Soon I'll start to hear a change'
(vii) 'I am singing low and high'
       'I am singing low and high'
(viii) 'Getting better as I try'
       'Getting better as I try'
(ix)   'I am learning everything'
       'I am learning everything'
(x)   'Cos I really love to sing'
       'Cos I really love to sing'
(xi)   'I'm developing my range'
       'I'm developing my range'
(xii) 'Soon I'll start to hear a change'
       'Soon I'll start to hear a change'
(xiii) 'When I'm singing at my best'
       'When I'm singing at my best'
(xiv) 'Even I will be impressed'
       'Even I will be impressed'

3. SUSTAINED VOWEL

(i)   E to OO
(ii)   E to OH
(iii) E to AH
(iv)   E to EH
(v)   E to OR

4. FURTHER PLACEMENT

–MAMA MIA FETTUCCINE

5. GLOTTAL ATTACK

(i)   EE, EE, EE, EE
(ii)   OO, OO, OO, OO
(iii) OH, OH, OH, OH
(iv)   AY, AY, AY, AY
(v)   EYE, EYE, EYE, EYE
(vi)   OR, OR, OR, OR
(vii) AH, AH, AH, AH

6. RANGE UP

(i)   HAVE A WONDERFUL DAY
(ii)   HAVE A MARVELLOUS DAY
(iii) HAVE A BEAUTIFUL DAY

7. ...RANGE DOWN – ON 'E'

8. OCTAVE JUMPS

a.   'AY'
b.   'OO'
c.   'EE'
d.   'OH'
e.   'AH'
f.   'OR'
g.   'I'
h.   'EH'

9. RANGE DOWN DARK - ON 'E'

10. CRESCENDO/DIMINUENDO

(i)   When people hear
(ii)   A voice they love
(iii)   It makes them feel
(iv)   Deep in their soul
(v)   As though the one
(vi)   Who has the voice
(vii)   Sings just for them
(viii) And them alone

11. VIBRATO

(i)	When people hear	NO VIB AT ALL
(ii)	A voice they love	SLOW VIB
(iii)	It makes them feel	FAST VIB
(iv)	Deep in their soul	NONE TO FAST VIB
(v)	As though the one	SLOW TO NO VIB
(vi)	Who has the voice	FAST TO SLOW VIB
(vii)	Sings just for them	NO TO SLOW TO FAST TO NO VIB
(viii)	And them alone	ANY COMBINATION YOU LIKE!

12. LIGHT AND SHADE

Loudly	Quietly
'YOU'RE WONDERFUL	'You're beautiful'
'YOU'RE WONDERFUL'	'You're beautiful"
'YOU'RE WONDERFUL'	'You're beautiful'
'YOU'RE WONDERFUL'	'You're beautiful'

13. FLEXIBILITY

Upwards	Downwards
'I'	'Love'
'It'	'When'
'You'	'Say'
'You'	'Like'
'My '	'Voice'
'It'	'Makes'
'Me'	'Feel'
'My'	'Work'
'Is'	'Done'

14. AD LIBBING

(i) Keep the words. Riff anywhere you like. Take your riffs up and downwards.

(ii) Now riff on the following words of the phrase.

Phrase No 1 - Riff on 'WON'
Phrase No 2 - Riff on 'YOU'RE'
Phrase No 3 - Riff on 'FUL'
Phrase No 4 - Riff on 'FUL'
Phrase No 5 - Riff on 'WON'
Phrase No 6 - Riff on 'YOU'RE'
Phrase No 7 - Riff on 'FUL'
Phrase No 8 - Riff on 'FUL'

(iii) Now take away all the words and phrasing and intricately riff to find all the unusual notes. It should sound very jazzy.

CONTENTS

INTRODUCTION

If you can speak you can sing. Whether you are looking to make a career in music, or simply enjoy singing, the aim of this book is to encourage you to explore your singing voice and increase your ability. With a little bit of application the sky's the limit. Every voice is unique and as vocal coaches the last thing we want is for you to sound like us or anyone else.

Whether you're a rocker, an R'n'B riffer or a classical diva we want to help you fulfil your natural talent. Your voice should be an expression of who you are and, as we all know, everyone is different. So it is with the voice.

Some chapters in this book deal with the preparation for a music industry career, others focus on vocal technique alone and still others on performance in general. This book is not designed to be read once only from start to finish. It should be a book you can dip into, read out of sequence – depending on your personal priorities – and revisit time after time as you grow to understand your own singing voice. We have also added a "Yes but" question here and there. As you learn there are always going to be questions so we have tried to include some of the most common ones we encounter.

PASSION

We have each worked in the industry for over 30 years and often people ask us how we remain excited about our work. We love music and we particularly love the sound of the human voice. Every individual and every voice is unique so, for us, each day is different. To see someone develop and change before your eyes is immensely gratifying. If you want to sing well you have to be passionate about it. One thing we never do after a coaching session is tell people they have to go away and practise. For one, most of the artists we work with would never be disciplined enough to do this, and two, they shouldn't be singing to please us. We feel an artist should be so inspired by what they are learning that they can't stop singing! Others should be telling them to, 'Shut up and be quiet'. Singing is the one career where you can legitimately love the sound of your own voice and get away with it!

What makes Michael Jackson take vocal coaching every day before recording? What makes Charlotte Church travel all the way from Wales for an hour and a half of vocal coaching with us in London? What makes Take That warm up to the CD in this book every night they have a gig? What makes Leona Lewis still take regular lessons? What makes Gwyneth Paltrow train every day for weeks before a performance? What makes Stevie Wonder put his production team on 24-hour standby just in case he wakes up at

3am and wants to record? What made Take That rehearse in the corridors of every TV station and studio up and down the country? What made Whitney Houston, at the height of her career, sit on the front row on several nights of a gospel tour in the hope she would be invited up on stage to sing? The answer is passion: the passion to sing; the passion for excellence.

GET READY FOR CHANGE

From our work with countless artists we know that the potential for discovery, progression and achievement is immense. Learning is like facing a series of mountains. You start with a sense of adventure and a goal: to reach the peak of the first mountain (it could be something as simple as learning to sing in tune). You achieve that goal, you feel euphoric and then you plateau. The plateau is followed by a feeling of discontent or even a lack of self-belief as you realise there is another mountain ahead, another task to be mastered. Many artists stop at this point, but true development means facing the next mountain and starting that long climb upward again. And so the cycle goes on and on. When you are down in the valley between mountains, it's important to remember that overall you are progressing and to remind yourself of what you have achieved so far.

Many of us expect immediate perfection when it comes to learning and it is important to realise achievement takes time. The end result will be a lot more satisfying when you have taken the time to enjoy the process.

Try not to be too hard on yourself. Ninety per cent of singing is about confidence and as you read on we hope you will gain the courage to leap off the mountain and go for it!

YES BUT: Why do I need to learn to sing. Isn't that for people who can't sing?

ANSWER: Many people go for years trying to hide the weaknesses in their voices, never knowing that a bit of technique could set their voice free. The voice develops throughout your whole life so working on it should help you embrace the changes, making the most of the instrument you have and helping you to navigate the transitions.

CHAPTER ONE

WHO ARE YOU?

I AM A PERSON AND A PRODUCT

Let's begin with your artistic identity. If you had to sell yourself where would you begin? If you were a product what would make the public choose you above another brand? What is your unique selling point (USP)? We know it sounds ruthless – and this book seeks to be affirming and positive about you as an individual – but as an artist in the commercial music industry these are the first questions any record company boss will have in his or her head the minute they lay eyes on you. Record companies are all different. Some are very creative, wanting to push back artistic boundaries or spend time developing talent; others are more like banks – sign it and get the product out there. Whatever their motivation and style the bottom line is they all need to make vast sums of money and you, the artist, hold the key to their fortune!

Simplicity is of the utmost importance when thinking about how you would market yourself. Your *music, voice and image* should all say the same thing. If you sing like a classical diva, look like a rocker and want to make hip hop music, the public will find it hard to catch on to you, to grasp what you're about. That's not to say there can never be a fusion of styles, but it has to be palatable, accessible and ultimately saleable.

ASK YOURSELF THE FOLLOWING QUESTIONS:

1. **WHAT MUSIC DO I MOST ENJOY?** Remember, it's you who's going to have to get out there and sing it night after night, twenty years down the line. If you hate it, you're going to have a very sad working life!

2. **WHAT DOES MY VISUAL IMAGE SAY ABOUT ME?** Are you a grungy guy, an opera babe, a hip hop rapper, a pop princess, an ageing rocker, a jazz man, a goth, a metaler, an indie chick, a disco diva or any other permutation?

3. WHAT TYPE OF MUSIC IS MY VOICE MOST SUITED TO? Artists make the most sense when their voice and their music match. Can you adapt your voice to suit the style of music you love to make? It will be easier for a record company or the general public to understand you and ultimately buy into you when the answers to these three questions begin to have some kind of linearity.

YES BUT: Can I A&R myself?

ANSWER: A&R stands for Artists and Repertoire, meaning the person who guides your musical style and the songs you write or choose to record. In this very exciting age of self-releasing, i-tunes, MySpace etcetera, etcetera, people are doing this all the time. You can perhaps reach 1,000 downloads if you are lucky, 10,000 even better, and this may launch a career; but it's important to remember it's not just about getting a track off the ground, it's about building a sustainable career. Keeping a constant perspective on your music is very difficult so if you are going to A&R yourself, we would recommend you surround yourself with a trustworthy team who can help guide your decisions.

GET YOUR PRIORITIES RIGHT

Using the three-circled model below ask yourself, as honestly as possible, what the public would first notice about you in order of importance. Is the point at which they are likely to connect with you your voice, your image or your music? All three need to be strong but you need to promote them in the order of their best quality. Inner circle – primary gift. Middle circle – secondary gift. Outer circle – reinforcement gift.

Chris Martin has a great image but it's his music that sold us on him. Lady Gaga has a good singing voice but it was her image we first picked up on. Amy Winehouse has a unique look but it's her singing voice we connected with first. What is your premier quality?

RE-ENFORCEMENT GIFT
SECONDARY GIFT
PRIMARY GIFT

Some people find it difficult to view themselves in a balanced way and alternate between thinking they are a demi-god or completely awful! It's much easier for producers and colleagues to work alongside you if everyone can be honest with you – and the honesty begins with you. When it comes to analysis and critique what you do and who you are should be kept as separate as possible. The quicker you develop the emotional skill to separate the two, the less pain you will have to endure. It's natural for an artist to be sensitive about their work because it's such a vulnerable, personal thing but try to create some distance between you and your art. Find someone you trust creatively and, using the three-circled model, get them to analyse you.

WHO ARE MY PEOPLE?

Another important question to ask yourself is, 'Who are my people?'. Are you the pre-teen pin-up, housewives' choice, the grannies' delight? Who is going to buy your music? Do you appeal to kids? Teens? Students? The twenty-somethings? The coffee table, dinner party thirties? The over-forties, with their disposable income? Do you have a particular group of people who will love your music? The R'n'B crowd? Middle-class rockers? The jazz lovers? It's not enough to say, 'Everyone'. You may well cross over into other areas but where do you start? Again, you could use the three-circled model to work out your demographic. Inner circle – target audience. Middle circle – broader audience. Outer circle – peripheral audience.

MANUFACTURED OR INNOVATIVE?

In our work we tend to categorise artists into two groups: the manufactured artist and the innovator.

The manufactured artist will generally have different motivation for being in the industry from that of the innovator. They may simply have a love of entertaining, not being too fussy about what kind of music they make as long as they have an audience. Many will not write their own material but will have teams of writer/producers who do this for them. They will be malleable, highly commercial and often have a desire just to be famous. They are usually great looking people who management and record companies know will have an immediate appeal in the press and on TV. Most pop music is made up of these people and their role in the music industry is to be totally respected.

The word 'manufactured' has come to have a derogatory emphasis. If 'manufactured' means an artist doesn't always write their own material, sings cover versions of songs and someone helped them to form their image then we must remember that, by this definition, we have to include Elvis, The Supremes, Alanis Morrisette, The Jacksons, Frank Sinatra and The Rolling Stones!

If an artist is pre-packaged and talentless that is one thing; if they are merely manufactured then they are indeed in good company!

The first question any child will ask on receiving a toy is, 'What does it do?'. People think being a celebrity is enough these days and in the short term that may be true. But in the long run, if you want to be an artist, you have to prove yourself. Are you looking for longevity? What is it you do? What makes you unique or different?

The innovator will be prepared to sit and make music in his/her bedroom even if no one gets to hear it. Money is not usually their motivation and although fame is a desire they will not be prepared to compromise their artistic beliefs for a short cut to success. They are harder to work with because they are not so easily manipulated but they are capable of magical moments of creativity. In the short term they will provide less immediate financial return for a record company than the manufactured artist but will generally have longer careers, focusing more on the album market than the singles market.

In summary: What are you good at? What kind of artist are you? Who will buy your music? Let the following chapters be filtered through this information.

MYSTERY AND THE UNKNOWN QUALITY

Record companies often say they are looking for someone with X factor to sign to their label. The X factor is an amalgam of different qualities that overall make up the unique identity of an artist. This can also mean different factors for each artist. The one thing we have noticed that these so called 'X factor' artists all have in common is mystery. Mystery is the quality that always leaves the audience wanting more. It makes the public hungry to read every magazine and newspaper article about them because no matter how much they tell you about themselves there always seems to be more to get to know. They also perpetuate this mystery by continually evolving so that just at the point where the audience has understood what the artist is all about, the artist has already moved on. The X factor artist never allows the audience to catch up.

CHAPTER TWO

PERFORMANCE – THE QUESTIONNAIRE

THE FOLLOWING TWO CHAPTERS are not so much about how to perform (we'll be covering that subject later) but why you perform.

Let's start with a questionnaire. Once a performer enters the public arena all sorts of questions are raised. Use the following to analyse where you are presently and to identify what you may need to work at changing.

QUESTION 1

You perform a gig and the response is amazing. They all love you. That is apart from one old school friend who says, 'I don't think you gave it your all'. Do you:

(A) Have a complete crisis of confidence? .... ☐

(B) Shake it off – it's only one person's opinion? .... ☐

(C) Tell yourself you've never liked the guy anyway and what does he know? .... ☐

QUESTION 2

A top music industry manager tells you they he may be interested in signing you but you have a day job. Do you:

(A) Say, 'Sorry, I can't get involved as I'm committed to my work and need to pay the rent'? .... ☐

(B) Stay in your job until things are a lot more concrete than just an interest? .... ☐

(C) Hand in your notice the next day – this is your moment and it needs every bit of your concentration? .... ☐

QUESTION 3

You're performing at a new venue with a new audience. Do you feel:

(A) Terrified – what if they hate you? .... ☐

(B) This is a challenge and new challenges are good? .... ☐

(C) If they hate you that's their problem – the venue's
grotty anyway? .... ☐

QUESTION 4

You and your song-writing partner write a great song. Friends seem to be crediting your partner and not you for its greatness. Do you:

(A) Think, 'This always happens. No one appreciates my role.'? .... ☐

(B) Feel OK – your song-writing partner and you both know
the reality of the situation and that's all that matters? .... ☐

(C) Feel angry with your song-writing partner and tell them
they should correct people if it happens again? .... ☐

QUESTION 5

Your Mum/Dad turns up at your recording session. Do you:

(A) Nervously watch them out of the corner of your eye the
whole time and try to judge what they are thinking? .... ☐

(B) Think, 'Hey, it's only a member of the family,' and make
them feel welcome? .... ☐

(C) Feel angry that they are interfering with your music
and consider asking them to leave? .... ☐

QUESTION 6

You and your friend are both auditioning for the same role. He/she gets the role and you lose out. Do you:

(A) Feel like giving up – everyone seems so much better than you? .... ☐

(B) Understand this wasn't the right role for you? .... ☐

(C) Tell your friend the role isn't a very good one and you'd be
unsure about taking it? .... ☐

QUESTION 7

You've had no work for ages and an offer comes in for a short-term singing job. The trouble is it's not your kind of music. Do you:

A Dither for so long that the job has gone when you ring back? .... ☐

B Take the job – you never know where it might lead and it is only short term?... ☐

C Turn the job down flat – you'd rather go hungry than compromise even one bit? .... ☐

QUESTION 8

Every time you and your band go on stage the guitarist upstages you. Do you:

A Make your performance smaller – you feel as if there's no room for two big performers up there? .... ☐

B Try to match your guitarist's performance so that the band looks even better? .... ☐

C Tell the guitarist to back off – you're the lead singer?..................... ☐

QUESTION 9

Two record companies offer you a deal. One completely understands your music, has a marketing budget but doesn't have a track record, the other doesn't view you as a priority, has a marketing budget and has a big track record. Do you:

A Sign to the company with the big track record? .... ☐

B Sign to the company with no track record knowing that they believe in you and you will give them the name they're looking for? .... ☐

C Don't sign to either – unless it's *all* right there's no point in signing to anyone?... ☐

QUESTION 10

Your family's out on a Karaoke night and your brother's just chosen the song you love to perform. Everyone loves it. Do you:

A Not bother to sing and say nothing?.. ☐

B Choose another song and congratulate your brother on his choice of song?... ☐

C Not sing and tell your brother not to choose your song the next time? .... ☐

MOSTLY 'As'

You compare yourself to others too much. You are easy to intimidate and lose confidence the minute something goes unexpectedly wrong. Try to keep a balanced perspective. Every person has their season and yours will come at the right time. You sometimes place your confidence in the hands of other people rather than your own. You need to take authority over what is yours and own it. If others don't appreciate what you have it doesn't matter. It's what you believe about yourself that matters.

You probably need to be a little more confrontational. Don't retreat.

MOSTLY 'Bs'

You have a balanced view of yourself. This is the attitude you need to survive happily in the music industry. (Many survive but not necessarily happily!) The knock-backs come but you keep your eyes on the final destination. You may lose a battle but you haven't lost the war. You allow others to have their opinions and you are able to co-exist with them even if their opinions conflict with yours.

MOSTLY 'Cs'

You are a natural rebel. Reject or be rejected is your motto. If criticism comes your way then you belittle the critic's credentials. Try to accept that not everybody will love you and that your audience IS out there. You are impulsive, easily offended and not afraid to confront angrily. Confrontation is a good thing if it leads to resolution.

Angry confrontation makes resolution hard. Try not to be unreasonable in your response to criticism.

Obviously, we should all be aiming towards the 'B' answers but we won't always achieve them and we are aware that not all situations are so straightforward. If you find yourself choosing the right answers more often then you are progressing. David and I have faced different versions of all of these situations and have very often reacted in a wrong way only to experience the painful consequences. By trial and error and by knowing what the right reaction should be we move forward and feel much better as a result.

CHAPTER THREE

PERFORMANCE – WHY?

OWNERSHIP

A great performer will make the audience feel totally comfortable and at ease because they pass on the confidence they feel to the viewer. Bluffing never works – if you don't believe it, they won't. An audience may not even know why they feel uncomfortable but they will detect a lack of self-belief in the performer. Only true self-belief puts an audience at ease.

We're not saying you have to be bursting with enthusiasm. If you are a shy performer you can work it to your advantage. If you are confident that it's OK to be shy then your audience will feel confident too and will probably love you for your understated style.

It all comes down to ownership. Who's in charge of the stage? Does the stage belong to the audience? Does it belong to the people who are employing you, to producers, management, agents or the people you need to impress? In truth, it belongs to none of the above. When you step up on to a stage there is only one person to whom that stage belongs and that is you. If you perform in a group then you have collective ownership. This may seem obvious to some but you would be surprised at how many artists have never thought about this subject and as a result their performances look apologetic, as though the audience has allowed them on to their space. They also tend not to use the whole stage, sticking to a small middle section where they feel most comfortable.

A great way to affirm your ownership is to walk all over your stage. Whether it's a rehearsal or performance space, before you start work, walk over the space and own it. Tell yourself it belongs to you for the time you are there. Walk out to the perimeters and look right across the space. It's yours and nobody else can have it while you are there. This is ownership. Ownership makes for commanding performances. With ownership comes a sense of authority. With authority comes responsibility.

AUTHORITY

OK, so now you own the space and know that you're in charge, let's ask the next question: Why are you there? Are you there for the audience or for yourself? After the ownership question many will say, 'For myself'.

Wrong! Sorry, but you're there for the audience. If you only want to please yourself that's fine, but stick to your living room. With authority comes responsibility. A performer may have loads of authority but if the performance is solely used to satisfy the performer it's selfish, unsatisfying to watch and it is a talent used irresponsibly. An artist who gives of him or herself, who truly pours themselves into their performance, is utterly captivating. Good performers are great at serving their audience.

You can really tell when a person wants to serve their audience. In all the singing competitions we have judged and taken part in, it is always interesting to see if the winner still takes coaching once they've won. For some it's enough to win and be famous; others want to make themselves even better for their audience. There is a hunger and thirst for improvement and an understanding that the audience matters.

A GIFT

It's sometimes helpful to view your talent as a gift. You have spent or will spend a lot of time honing your voice, sharpening your skills and making them into a beautiful gift-wrapped present. When you get up on stage you take your present with you and as you perform you unwrap it for the audience to see and enjoy. If the audience doesn't like your gift that's their problem – your responsibility is to give it.

Carrie and I sometimes try to view our gifts as not belonging to us but rather something we have been entrusted with. We are 'The Agents' if you like and we represent the talents housed in us. 'Selling yourself' is one of the hardest things about being in the music industry but when the ownership of your talents is not quite so closely connected to you it's much easier.

When you give a present to someone you always hope they are going to love it, especially if you have spent a lot of time preparing it. When it's unwrapped and they love what you have given this, in turn, gives you a deep sense of satisfaction. The primary joy should always remain in the giving of the gift. Love what you do, not the response you get. If your priorities change for the worse you will be in danger of becoming what we call an applause junkie – someone who only ever lives for the response of the audience. Like all addictions, after a while the artist hates performing as the applause is never quite enough and they can't wait for the next hit. Artists who have this attitude are a nightmare to be around because it's 'all about them'. There is nothing better than a grateful artist.

We have seen this powerfully in the boys from Take That. Because they have been given a second chance, they are grateful for every minute they get to spend in the limelight.

APPROVAL

Artists are brave people. Every time they step on to a stage they run the risk of being laughed at, hated and rejected. It's a very hard position to be in. Ruby Wax has a great saying: 'Dysfunction breeds the need for celebrity.' This is so true. Many approval-hungry people are attracted to the music industry. For them, the possibility of adoration from a large number of complete strangers is worth performing for. Night after night they will take the risk of humiliation in the hope of receiving the love of their audience. The love of a bunch of strangers is far more appealing and less risky than entering into personal relationships where people can hurt and wound. For many who already hurt, the performing arts, with their impersonal adoration, are magnetic. Try as hard as you can to keep the need for approval far away from the joy of your performance. Your performance will be freed up when you do. None of us has completely pure motives but for your own sense of well-being it's better to deal with some of these issues before embarking on a career in the performing arts.

STAGE FRIGHT

A person's fear of performing is normally tied up in one or more of the areas we have spoken about earlier in this chapter. We have worked with many artists who experience stage fright and have worked through some of their fears with them. Talking to a trustworthy listener always helps you to process some of your thoughts.

Visualisation – This is a technique some people find useful when dealing with stage fright. It's a massive subject and we are not looking to explore all its uses in this book but the basics can be very helpful.

1   Imagine you are backstage and you have a confidence deposit box inside you and it is empty.
2   Imagine filling the deposit box up with confidence. From the tip of your toes to the top of your head and especially over your voice.
3   Imagine walking out on to the stage.
4   Look at the audience.
5   Tell yourself the audience is not one enormous giant but a series of individuals and that your confidence deposit box is still full. If it needs refilling then imagine filling it up again.
6   Tell yourself you *can* sing to this audience.
7   Tell yourself they cannot hurt you, that they are there to enjoy your performance.
8   Imagine all the important things that matter in your life and tell yourself that, putting everything in perspective, this really isn't the thing that matters to you most.
9   Say hello to the audience. Tell them they are welcome into your space and you hope they like what you have brought for them.
10 Imagine walking off stage and imagine the confidence deposit box still full.

When you arrive at the venue go through this process again. Even walk through the audience space and tell yourself it's OK. Whatever issue you may have, know that many have gone before you with exactly the same issues and many have succeeded in dealing with them.

YES BUT: I don't have any of these issues.

ANSWER: It always worries us when people claim they have none of these issues. The older we get, the more issues we are aware of. The subject of this chapter (why we do what we do) is a conundrum. It is something that will probably take a lifetime of working through! Try to be open to growth and honesty. Success brings power and that is a very dangerous thing in the hands of the wrong person. Most of all because, ultimately, it destroys the person who wields the power.

CHAPTER FOUR

HOW THE VOICE WORKS – PHYSIOLOGY AND PROBLEMS

THE HUMAN VOICE is the most fascinating instrument of all. Much has been written about the physiology of the voice and it is our aim to keep it as simple as possible. A lack of knowledge can result in easily avoidable damage being done but we also believe too much technical information can be stifling to the singer who simply wants to begin to enjoy his or her voice. If you want to know more about the physical side of the throat, voice box, larynx and so on we recommend you check out a good anatomy book. We are going to look at the areas that will help you to reinforce the technique we teach further on in this book.

It is absolutely imperative that you use your voice correctly. If you do not, with overuse you may begin to have all sorts of throat illnesses, nodules, polyps, etc. It's simple: bad technique leads to throat problems.

THE VOCAL CORDS

As we can see from the picture there are two folds of muscle resting in the centre of the larynx. These are the vocal cords. They have three functions. Firstly, they control the flow of air going in and out of the lungs. Their second function is to protect the airway. The third function – and the one that interests us – is that as air passes through them the edges produce sound for either

Healthy vocal cords

speech or singing. They work on an involuntary basis, drawing together with the intention of speaking or singing. They vibrate together slowly for low notes and quickly for high notes.

The vocal cords are covered by a thin layer called mucosa, which produces mucous. This mucous keeps the vocal cords lubricated. Smoking and ill health often affect the mucous production of these glands. If you want to take care of your voice please try not to smoke. We have worked with people who literally sing and smoke at the same time. As the cords are drawn together to produce sound you can imagine what affect the dry smoke of the cigarette is having on the surface of the cords.

There are other cords above the main vocal cords. These are known as the secondary cords or 'false' cords. Some singers use these cords when they speak and if they do they often find they also use them for singing. This can lead to all sorts of problems and we normally recommend speech therapy before learning singing technique, as speech is usually where the problem has begun.

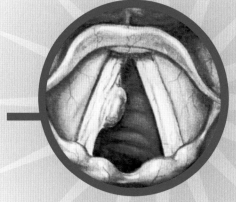

Vocal cords with a nodule on each corresponding side

Vocal injury - this occurs initially when the vocal cords swell as a result of bad technique. If misuse continues the swellings can become nodules, which basically means the tissue has hardened. When looking at the vocal cords the classic nodule picture is of a spot on each corresponding side of the cords. Normally nodules are treated with speech therapy and they go away. Occasionally surgery may be advisable.

We would always recommend that you get a second opinion on throat issues. We have met so many people who have been mis-diagnosed, told they have nodules, for example, when they have a different problem. Been given no therapy or treatment at all. Just told to rest when what they really need is to know how to prevent a recurrence. Voice therapy and developing good technique is far more advisable than surgery – there is no guarantee that the voice will be the same after surgery has been performed on the vocal cords.

Vocal cysts are also common but these are not usually caused by bad technique. They often appear on one side of the cords only and they are caused by one of the glands that cover the cords not draining properly. Voice therapy will not usually work on a cyst and it normally has to be removed surgically.

There are also problems when the vocal cords develop a polyp. This is not normally caused by bad technique, but by reflux or smoking. The person will probably speak with a hoarse sound to their voice. The polyp is normally just

Polyps often appear on one side of the chords

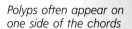

on one side but can be on both sides of the cords. It is usually a soft, broad-based swelling that is more blister-like and larger than the harder nodule. It is generally dealt with by surgery.

During *Fame Academy* we had to let one of our students go due to throat problems. I knew there was an issue the moment I heard her speak. Her voice was raspy and airy and she could produce no clear sound when either speaking or singing. If you can imagine your vocal cords being drawn together to produce a sound and in their way is a spot on each side. Air escapes either side of the spot making the person unable to give a clear sound.

Many people have airy voices but if you have absolutely no ability to produce a clear sound – whether in speech or in singing – then it's worth having your throat looked at. If your voice sometimes sounds a bit airy but most of the time it's completely clear the chances are you just need to develop good technique and you don't have a big problem.

Similarly, some singers begin to lose a note from the middle of their range. If the note changes from one day to another the chances are you just haven't mastered the technique needed to achieve the notes. If you always have the same note missing it may be advisable to have your throat examined. To summarise: if the vocal problem is consistent it's more likely that something is wrong than if it is intermittent. We advise all our students to get their voices checked out regularly.

Most singers we have coached who have had problems have developed those problems during the early days of their careers. Singing in venues with bad sound systems has made them over-sing in order to hear themselves. Pushing the voice night after night like this is a recipe for disaster. When you stand in front of a drum kit and sing you need proper amplification. Physiologically your voice is at its fittest and fullest around your mid-thirties, so don't destroy it in a club at sixteen!

CHAPTER FIVE

HOW TO KEEP THE VOICE HEALTHY

WHEN A SINGER has not slept, has a poor diet or has drunk too much alcohol or caffeine it shows in the voice almost immediately. If you have over-sung or your throat feels tired or you have a bad cold there are a few things you can do.

REMEDIES

Sleep – This is the best healer for a tired voice. Rest the voice and try not to speak unless absolutely necessary. Some people try whispering as it seems less brutal than speaking but in truth it pushes the cords together in a harder way than clear speech. Keep the volume down and keep the voice clear. Better still, try writing!

Atmosphere – Stay in a well-ventilated room away from draughts and sudden temperature changes. Try a humidifier to keep the moisture in the air. A dry atmosphere is not good for the throat. Keep away from smoky rooms.

Warmth – If you are going from place to place where you have sudden temperature changes wear a scarf around your neck. A lot of performers come off stage sweating and run out into the cold to get on the tour bus and often they are still wearing the flimsy clothes they were wearing on stage. Grab a scarf.

Fluids – Keep up your fluid intake. It re-hydrates your whole body. Steer away from ice- cold or fizzy drinks. Room-temperature water is best. Just imagine what happens when your vocal cords are nicely warmed up and then you chuck freezing cold water all over them. It's like going for a jog and then jumping into a freezing lake! Your expanded muscles will tell you about it. Alcohol is OK as long as it's in moderation but try to avoid it if you have a throat problem. Alcohol dehydrates the body so drink plenty of water with it.

Steaming – We recommend a ten-minute steam, twice a day when you are using your voice a lot, if your voice is tired or if you have a cold. Phlegm is a nightmare to move if it thickens and sticks to the cords. Steam inhalation helps to get it moving. Put one teaspoon of Friars Balsam (you can buy this quite cheaply from most local chemists) into one pint of hot water. Rest your head over the bowl, placing a towel over your head and the bowl to stop the steam escaping. Don't put your face in the water or you may burn it. (N.B. Friars Balsam is a sticky substance that's hard to remove so use a bowl you don't need fwor anything else.)

Diet – Try to eat foods that have a high water content, such as fresh fruit and vegetables. Try to avoid dairy products as they induce phlegm, e.g. cheese and chocolate.

Throat lozenges – These should only be used when the singing voice is out of use, i.e. when you are resting and not about to sing. Most throat lozenges work in two ways. They soothe and they anaesthetise. The soothing aspect is fine but imagine you have a sore throat and you take a lozenge before you sing. This is what happens: you anaesthetise the throat and more often than not push the voice and sing as though the problem isn't there. Later, when the anaesthetic effect has worn off, your throat hurts even more. Remember that the pain in your throat is an indicator that something is wrong. Masking the pain and then pushing your voice will make matters far worse.

Remedy drink – A good drink to have if your voice is tired is a mixture of one teaspoon of honey, one teaspoon of lemon and a couple of slices of fresh ginger mixed together in hot water. The honey soothes, the lemon cuts through phlegm and the ginger acts as a natural anti-inflammatory, helping to take down any swelling.

Warm-up – When you feel your voice is sufficiently rested try a gentle warm up, starting with humming. Do not push your voice or go to the outer perimeters of your range straight away. Taking things slowly and gradually is important.
Be patient if you cannot achieve your usual vocal range. If you have had a throat problem it can take time to regain your usual vocal stamina.

Whatever you do to maintain your voice or help it heal remember that good technique is the best preventative medicine you can apply.

SHOULD I SING IF I HAVE A COLD?

This depends on the type of cold you have. There seem to be a lot of symptoms that we put under the heading of having a cold.

Chest cold – You should try to avoid singing if you have a cold on your chest. Phlegm is likely to be brought up through to the cords and if it is sticky it will rest on them.

Blocked nose – You should still be able to sing with a blocked nose. The technique we use should allow your blocked nose to go almost undetected. If your nose is completely blocked you may sound a little nasal.

Headache – If you have a headache it may hurt you to sing as the vibration of the voice fills the head cavity but the sound you produce should not be affected.

Earache – If you have earache you should still be able to sing. However, if your ears are blocked then you may have problems with your tuning.

Gritty sore throat – You can sing with a sore throat but you must be careful not to push your voice too much. Keep all speaking and singing to a minimum. If your voice does not sound as clear and full as it normally would you may find yourself pushing the voice in order to get the sound out. This causes swelling or inflammation of the cords so beware.

Laryngitis – This is the inflammation of the vocal chords. Do not even attempt to sing if you have laryngitis. Rest the voice and if it persists visit your doctor for advice.

Thick phlegm – If the phlegm is on the move you should be OK as you will either swallow or blow it out through your nose. If it is sticking on your throat you may struggle to sing.

Sinus problems – You should be able to sing as normal. If you are taking antihistamine medicine make sure you keep up your intake of water as the medicine can make your cords dry. For blocked nose see above.

Cough – You should still be able to sing with a persistent or chesty cough. Sometimes the coughing abates as you sing. As we have said before, try not to push the voice if it doesn't seem to have its normal sound or power.

CLEARING YOUR THROAT

When singers clear their throats by coughing it can cause all sorts of vocal problems. The best way to get round the situation is to swallow. It takes a while to discipline yourself to swallow rather than cough but you save yourself so much hassle by doing so.

VOICE BREAKING

As boys reach their early- to mid-teens their bodies release testosterone. This causes the cartilage of the larynx to grow and thicken and it begins to stick out. This is the Adam's Apple. The vocal cords also grow longer and thicker by about sixty per cent with the result that they vibrate at a slower rate and at a lower frequency. The face grows and as the cavities enlarge this space causes the voice to sound deeper. Most people don't realise that girls' voices also break but they only drop in range by about two to four notes whereas boys' voices drop about an octave so it is more noticeable.

A lot has been said about the voice breaking but let's get rid of a few myths. Firstly, not all boys' voices break suddenly overnight. Normally it happens over a period of months. Secondly, and most importantly, it doesn't mean you will never sing again! We encourage boys to continue singing during the period when the voice is in transition and to keep up with their training and we've seen tremendous results from those who do.

SHOUTING

Whenever we have been called out during a tour because an artist is having vocal problems we have nearly always found the same root cause. You watch a show, they are applying their technique in a healthy way and then they get to the end of the song and scream, 'Hello, Wembley!'. Then they tell you they have been doing interviews for four hours prior to the concert and suddenly everything makes sense!

Many singers have very good technique when it comes to singing but when they speak they raise and push their voice. A microphone will carry your voice and it is absolutely possible to sound excited without screaming!

These days many singers are choosing to have periods of no speaking to give the voice a total rest and some singers will not talk at all on the day of a gig. Know your voice – if this is what it takes, then do it.

YES BUT: I love my gravely voice. Won't technique take it away?

ANSWER: This is a really tricky one. Technique should strengthen what's already there. In our experience, singers with this tone need a good solid technique which will under-gird the voice and strengthen the vocal cords.

YES BUT: I can belt my voice out all day and night and my throat doesn't hurt.

ANSWER: Every voice is different. Some people have naturally strong voices and others more fragile. Like a good work out, technique is good for all. Some voices seem to be able to take alcohol, cigarette smoke, late nights and never give up. In our experience these voices are rare exceptions. A young voice is often strong but it's a dangerous thing to think it will last forever. Often you'll hit late teens and early twenties and suddenly all the tone has gone on the voice and it sounds tired.

CHAPTER SIX

LEARNING HOW TO LEARN

BEFORE WE GET STARTED on the technical stuff it's worth asking yourself the questions: 'What is my attitude toward learning? What am I expecting to gain and how quickly am I expecting to achieve my goals?'

BLOCKS TO LEARNING

Teaching begins from babyhood up. If nothing short of perfection was acceptable from you as a child then you will probably have a perfectionist attitude to learning. If you have been given rigid, uninspiring teaching at school the chances are you will think of the learning process as pointless and credit all you know to your own life experiences. We often teach people whose problem is not with singing but with learning.

Perfectionism – Demanding perfect results first time is not helpful. You will always feel you are failing.

DAVID: As a child I loved playing the piano. To begin with I'd practise new pieces of music for hours until I'd learned them by heart. Then I started with a new teacher who thought I learned things by heart because I couldn't read the music properly. She would ask me to play unfamiliar exercises and if I didn't get them note perfect first time she would rap me across the knuckles with a wooden ruler. The result of this was I began to hate my piano lessons, I stopped practising and within a year I'd given up. Even today, when I sit at the piano I have to overcome the fear of playing a wrong note. Perfectionist teaching leads to unconfident, perfectionist students. Go easy on yourself.

Pride – Proud people are usually deeply insecure people. Often proud artists have a 'shut down' attitude to learning. They think what they know is enough to get through so why should they bother to learn any more? Learning is a magical, freeing experience – and it never ends. There is never a point at which you can say 'I know everything about my voice'. The voice is constantly changing and evolving and as you choose to discover it, the adventure begins. Pride stunts growth.

Fear – Fear is another big barrier to learning. Fear of the unknown; fear that you may not be good enough; fear of change; fear of confronting the magnitude of what you may not know. In the context of singing and grasping artistic skills, change is good. You are not being asked to solve the world's problems, you are merely presented with the small task of grasping your own voice. If you fear you may not be very good you must first learn to enjoy your singing for yourself before wondering what other people may say. If you constantly listen to your voice as though you were a third party you will never take risks and never fully grow. Do it for YOU first.

Comparison – It is not good to compare constantly either your potential or your progress with another. General comparison can be helpful but constant analysis can be crushing to a student. Remember, you are unique and your voice is unique.

THE TIGHTROPE AND THE FIELD

Whatever you struggle with (and we are sure there are many other struggles apart from those listed) try not to let it be a block to your learning. If you stay locked in these modes it's like walking on a tightrope. After a while just trying to stay on is difficult as the necessity of learning new things pulls you in different directions and threatens your balance. The truth is learning should free you; it should put you in a spacious place. It should give you the opportunity to run around 'the field'.

Taking time – In this quick-fix, fast-food world we live in it is very tempting to demand instant results from yourself. If we do not achieve straight away we swiftly move on to something else. Don't worry if learning seems to be taking a long time. The learning process cannot be rushed or you will end up confused and be more likely to give up.

CARRIE: When I began my career I started out as a dancer. I was the slowest learner on every job. All the dancers would be going through the steps ten to the dozen and I would be in the corner trying to grasp the first two movements and put them together. I was only sixteen and I would so easily lose my confidence. I spent most of those days as a dancer feeling that the other dancers thought I was stupid. The important thing to remember (and I wish someone had said this to me back then) is that when you are on stage none of the audience is judging the performance based on how quickly you learned the routine. It's better to have great style and be a slow learner than to be a quick learner but have no style!

We're sure you know the story of the hare and the tortoise. Both start the race but the hare knows he is very fast so he stops for a rest just short of the finishing line. He knows he's safe as the tortoise won't be around for a while. In the meantime the tortoise slowly makes his way round the course, passes the sleeping hare and takes the winning prize. This story parallels the music industry closely. We often meet averagely talented people who have worked so hard that they have clawed their way to the top of the ladder. Equally, the bottom of the ladder is littered with massively talented artists who have simply not bothered to learn. Natural talent can prove to be a great hindrance to learning. Being a great artist is ten per cent inspiration and ninety per cent perspiration, so discipline yourself to learn.

PROCESS VS GOAL

The culture we live in is very goal-orientated. Employees are very often judged by results alone. Those results are often figures and sums as opposed to feelings and influence. Feelings and influence are much harder to judge and yet they are central to the overall impact. So it is with learning. Hitting the highest note possible or doing all the vocal gymnastics in the world does not make a great singer. Learning to enjoy the process is a fantastic experience.

One of the greatest producer/writer/arrangers of our time is Quincy Jones. He tells a great story about how he views his time in the music industry.
He compares the music industry to a park. He says some people walk into the park and head straight for the gate on the other side. Others stop to smell the flowers and take in the atmosphere. In his career he chose the latter way to cross the park and says he has enjoyed the experience very much.

Remember: we are human beings not human doings. It's not just about achievement; it's about enjoying the process and just being.

Bad Habits – Bad habits can be hard to break. In counselling terms they say it takes six weeks to break a habit. In your singing there will be areas you feel secure with and we may be asking you to let go of them. Try to have the courage and trust to let go and embrace new teachings. You have nothing to lose.

When singers say, 'I don't need teaching. I like the sound of my voice,' what they usually mean is, 'I'm insecure about my voice and I don't want to know that I might be doing something wrong,' or, 'I do what I know and I don't want to know anything new'.

Self-talk – Self-talk is that voice or conversation that goes on almost constantly in our heads. If we are to progress as artists it is essential that we discipline our self-talk. A constant stream of negative words going through our heads telling us we cannot do this or we will never achieve that has an amazingly profound effect upon our progress. We teach some artists and as we encourage them you can tell in their heads they are contradicting the praise they are receiving. Try to be balanced. If you have a long way to go it doesn't matter so long as you are progressing within yourself. Start answering back to your self-talk!

CARRIE: A few years ago I was called in for a singing session to sing backing vocals for Bette Midler. On the first day Bette wasn't needed but the musicians and singers were recording the backing track in a studio in London. Throughout the session a dapper old man stood in the corner, ignored and almost unobserved. He looked as if he belonged in an over-sixties club and not a recording studio. As the session drew to a close he came over and introduced himself. His name? Arif Mardin.

This was a man who had produced some of the biggest hits of all time: Aretha Franklin's 'You Make Me Feel Like A Natural Woman', Bette Midler's 'Wind Beneath My Wings', Chaka Khan's 'I Feel For You' and the Nora Jones album. He' had also worked with the Bee Gees, The Smashing Pumpkins, Isaac Hayes and Dusty Springfield. And he'd won six Grammys! He was a musical demi-god! His story was fascinating. He lived in Turkey before attending the London School of Economics. He was a great lover of jazz music and when he was in his late twenties he decided it was time to fulfil his dream to study music. Quincy Jones had just started a scholarship scheme to the Berklee Music School and Arif Mardin won the first ever Quincy Jones scholarship. It was meant to be for school leavers but against all the odds Arif won the award.

When you are determined there is no end to what you can achieve.

CHAPTER SEVEN

PREPARING FOR YOUR LESSON

SAFE SPACE

It's important to recognise that the four walls within which you learn and rehearse are your 'safe space'. Allow yourself to make mistakes. Progress can only be achieved when you are willing to take your voice beyond where it has been before. This means letting go of some of the old and embracing something new. Many turn back at this stage because they only want to sound good. Remember: sometimes you have to let go of the good and go through sounding average in order to achieve something great. Magical singing moments happen when you take risks and step into the unknown.

Many artists we work with have not had this creative, safe space when growing up. How many children, when enjoying their own singing, have heard those immortal words from their parents, 'Shut up. Your noise is driving me mad'? (Or something to that effect?) Many people who grow up with this continual response to their singing only ever feel safe singing alone, where no one can hear or comment. They will never risk singing in front of an audience. If this has been your experience we suggest you develop your safe space first and when you have learned to feel confident and enjoy your singing, then consider taking it to a wider audience.

Experimenting with your voice is an essential part of the process. We regularly witness singers howling their way through a lesson only to hear a stunning performance on the very same night. Why? Because they feel safe to experiment, knowing that if they try ten new things that don't sound good they may discover one that does. They can then take that one out of their 'safe space' and perform it to a wider audience.

WATER AND A MIRROR

Many singers like to have a glass of water to sip during their session. If you need to have a drink of water make sure it is at room temperature or warm – never ice cold – and also make sure it is still and not fizzy. Try to sip and not gulp down lots of water or even try a water spray (Evian make one). A mirror is also a handy aid as you will be able to check yourself regularly.

REST TIME

A time of intensive training should be followed by a period of rest and this is a repeated cycle. The rest is as important as the training. You need to take time to let the teaching sink in and filter through every aspect of what you already know. When we have scripts or songs to learn it's amazing how at midnight we haven't got a clue what we are doing and then first thing in the morning we can suddenly recite our script word-perfect. Rest is a good thing. To begin with you probably need to keep training quite intensively, but later on a period away from learning can be a good thing.

DIFFERENT TEACHING TECHNIQUES

Different teachers teach different techniques. It isn't necessarily the case that some are wrong and others right. We each take a different approach to get what we think sounds good and is safe. If you have had a number of different singing teachers you will notice they sometimes seem to contradict each other. Our advice is that you should take what is helpful for you. As coaches we feel that we are there to offer you a handful of keys. Some you may wish to ignore and others you will use to unlock your voice and begin a journey. Where one person has been struggling with breath control another's struggle may be with increasing their vocal range. Hopefully this book will cover most of the main areas needed for development.

YOU HOLD THE KEYS

Remember: we hand you the keys but you have to open the door. You are actively involved in the process all the way along. No teacher can magic you into becoming a brilliant singer. It comes down to you applying what you are learning. You can learn to sing if you are prepared to take the time to learn. For some who are just starting out it will mean learning to hold a tune, for others it will mean going from an amateur to a professional status, and for others still it will mean going from very good to magical singing performances. Whatever you need the same technique applies to all. You take and apply it to your own personal level.

SOLID FOUNDATION

The technique we teach is to be used as the foundation for all the different singing styles you may like to use. It involves breathing and placement. We will explain just what these terms mean later but they are the bedrock upon which you add your vocal identity, all the colours of the voice and interpretation skills. Many singers are all style and no substance. Their voices have loads of identity, clever pronunciation, intricate choices of notes and yet their voices lack body. There is no fullness to the sound because they are just using a series of affectations. It's like the tip of the iceberg without the ninety per cent beneath the surface that supports it. It is essential to have a solid foundation upon which to build your own 'sound' and identity.

DIAGNOSIS

Learning to diagnose your vocal problems is something that takes time and experience. As you begin the singing journey you will find you will get to know your voice better and as you do you will be able to tell where it is lacking and where it is progressing, where it is tired and where it's out of shape.

LISTENING

The sound you hear in your head when you sing is totally different from the voice that everyone else hears. This is because we hear our voice through the bones of the skull and on to our eardrums so it sounds louder and fuller.

It may take time for you to judge your own sound but practise helps. If you are a recording artist you will have the advantage of being able to hear yourself back and change your voice accordingly.

STAGES IN TECHNIQUE COACHING

When we are teaching technique we aim to take our students through a number of stages.

TRAINING is the first stage, where we are discovering the voice and a lot of time is spent demonstrating and diagnosing the problem areas.

COACHING is the second stage, where artists are learning how to diagnose their own problems and correct themselves accordingly. There is less demonstration and more calling out from the sidelines!

MAINTENANCE is where an artist knows his or her voice from start to finish and it is our job then to maintain and to help with any problems or changes the singer has to incorporate as the voice develops with age and experience.

Obviously, we are not able to take every reader through this process but it may be helpful to know the stages you have to go through in the learning process.

In the early days the chapters on technique (the 'Implementation' section of the book) should be a constant companion during your exercises. As you progress you will probably need to concentrate more on the 'Paint Palette' chapter and finally the 'How To Sell A Song' and 'Performance' chapters. Remember always to refer back so that you take your foundational technique with you as you build. Bad habits sometimes recur so it's good to go back and check yourself. Sometimes a particular piece of information that has little relevance first time round may be a transforming key for you later on.

WHAT SHOULD A LESSON CONTAIN?

A lesson should have a balance of technique, interpretation and performance. You will notice from the different chapters of this book that all these areas are covered. Many singing teachers stick just to technique, while others concentrate on how to interpret songs. But it is always our aim to give the student a well-rounded lesson containing all three vital components to the singing experience. Good, healthy technique (both in exercises and songs) followed through with learning how best to interpret a song vocally and finally the physical and facial delivery.

YES BUT: Can I really learn from a book in the same way as I can learn from a teacher?

ANSWER: There is nothing as helpful as being able to stand and sing in front of a good coach. However, we do believe learning from a book can still unlock your voice. It can also be used as a great back-up between lessons, especially if your lessons are not weekly.

CHAPTER EIGHT

TECHNIQUE — BREATHING

HOW SHOULD I STAND?

Let's start with how you should stand when singing. The most important thing to remember is RELAX! Look at the diagram on the right.

Notice the body is straight with shoulders down. The head is looking forward and the neck muscles are not contorted or strained in any way. The chin is relaxed and even. (We'll talk about the jaw when we come to the section on placement teaching.) Even the tongue should be relaxed!

The face – When it comes to singing properly, pained expressions should only come as a performance choice, not because of the pain we are suffering as a result of trying to get the notes out. So relax your face and let your voice do the talking!

8

BREATHING

Good breath control is essential if we are to sing safely and with any power. Breathing affects the sound projection. You may have heard about the diaphragm being used for singing. Let's take a look at what happens when you breathe.

The diaphragm is positioned just underneath the lungs. In its resting position during exhalation it is in a convex position. As you breathe in the diaphragm moves downward into a concave position to make room for the lungs to fill with air. It moves on an involuntary basis so you cannot make it move other than with inhalation.

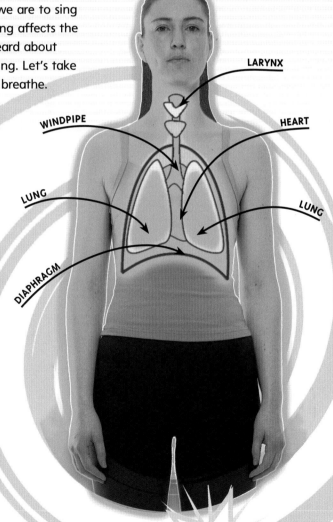

LARYNX

WINDPIPE

HEART

LUNG

LUNG

DIAPHRAGM

A BRIEF HISTORY OF DIAPHRAGMATIC BREATHING

During the Victorian era it became popular to have an upright piano in the home and 'nice girls' were taught to sing and play. Think about the fashions of the day. Ladies were wearing the tightest bodices imaginable and so it followed that all the teaching they received on breathing was focused on the upper torso. As a result many people erroneously believe that it is the diaphragm alone that supports the voice when in fact the real support starts a lot lower down – in an area considered quite unmentionable back in those days!

The lower abdominal muscles are the unsung heroes of singing. It is ultimately they that kick and control the air out of the lungs. If you breathe in a certain way when speaking the same should apply when you are singing. The hard thing to do is not to go into a special 'this is my breathing for singing' type of breathing – as many singers do. The shoulders go up, the chest rises out of all proportion and the abdominal muscles are left taut. If you have a dancing background or are into fitness you will be particularly prone to this. As dancers move their arms around all the time they tend to breathe in a very shallow way, using the upper chest only. Dancing while singing is a hard skill to master and to do it well the lower abdominal muscles must come into play.

The lower abdominal muscles should relax on inhalation (breathing in). This means that when you breathe out or sing the muscles will contract, pushing the air out and controlling its flow. In fact when you are using all the lower muscles even your bottom tightens as you get to the last remnants of breath!

Put your hand just below your tummy button or tuck it in your waistband.

Breathe IN THROUGH THE NOSE, relaxing the tummy muscles, and slowly breathe OUT THROUGH THE MOUTH. Try it a few times – it may take a while to co-ordinate.

In these 'flat as a wash-board tummy' days we live in it goes against all our thinking to relax the abdominal muscles. But if we are to support the voice we must begin to do so.

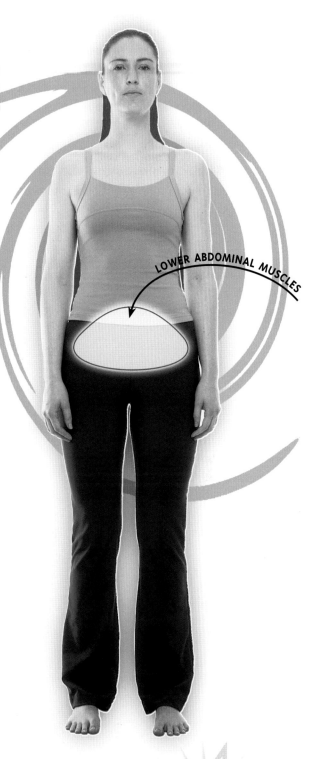

LOWER ABDOMINAL MUSCLES

As we said earlier, singing is an extension of speaking. Try this: imagine someone has picked up your purse/wallet by mistake. They are walking away at quite a rate and you need to stop them. Keeping your hand on your lower abdomen, breathe in, relaxing the abdominal muscles and call out, 'Hey! Come back'. Check what happens. If you relaxed your muscles during inhalation you will find they went hard as you called out. This also happens when you laugh and when you cry and the same process should happen as you sing. If you want your singing voice to have power and strength these muscles have to get involved.

It is also interesting to note the width of your lower torso compared with the width of your neck (see diagram on the right). It is much safer to put the support of your voice on to this area rather than on to your throat. If you have a big voice and a little body it's even more important to make sure you are supporting your voice properly by literally 'putting body' into the sound.

Relaxing these lower bands of abdominal muscles is the quickest and easiest way to take the big breaths that are necessary for singing. If you have ever been to watch opera you will notice the singers are able to hit very high notes

Opera singers support their voices by using their bodies to control their breath. This enables them to hit high notes even when lying down.

while throwing themselves around the stage. This is because they are supporting their voices by using their bodies to control the breath.

SINGING SHOULD NEVER HURT. If it does you are doing it wrong. The only thing that should feel tired after a singing session is your abdomen from all the breathing!

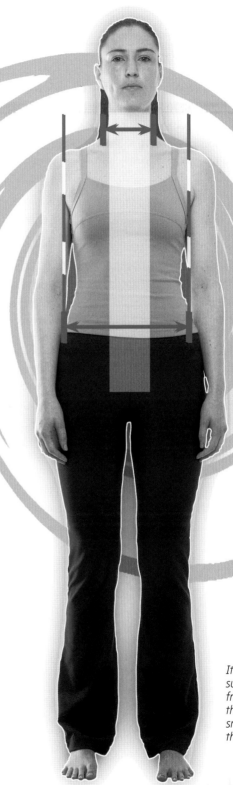

It is much safer to support your voice from your lower torso than from the much smaller area of your throat.

BREATHING EXERCISES

Exercise 1

Relaxing your shoulders (it may be helpful to check your posture in your mirror), breathe in through the nose, relaxing the abdominal muscles as you do so. The air should fill your lungs to the point where you feel even the back of your ribcage opening up. Slowly breathe out through the mouth, controlling the flow of air. Do not lift your shoulders or stick your chest out. This should look as relaxed as speaking! A lot of singers release lots of air at the start of exhalation and this follows through when they are singing notes. Try to breathe out in an even and measured way. REPEAT ten times.

You may find you are feeling a little dizzy. This is what we term an 'oxygen rush'. If this happens stop and breathe at a normal rate and then begin again. If you feel really dizzy take a seat for a couple of minutes. Sometimes we have had singers start to sway as they are breathing. Don't be so enthusiastic that you nearly faint before stopping. It isn't a competition!

Exercise 2

Breathe in, as above, but this time we are going to breathe out in stages. Slowly release some air then stop. Count to three (but don't breathe in again). Release a little more air then stop again. Count to three. Release a little more air then stop. Count to three and then finally release any air you have left. REPEAT five times.

It may take a while to achieve this many stops as you may run out of breath too soon. You will get better with practise. Build up your breath control by releasing the air more slowly. After a while you may wish to add more stops.

Exercise 3

Breathe in, relaxing the abdominal muscles as before. This time place your index finger in front of your mouth, as though you were asking someone to be quiet, and slowly hiss on 'S' as you exhale. Hear how even or uneven the breath is. REPEAT five times.

If at first the hissing sounds uneven do persevere, you will quickly begin to notice the difference in how even the airflow becomes. The consistency in the hissing sound is an indication of how controlled your breathing is. The more you progress with your singing, the more essential breath control becomes. You can increase your lung capacity by doing aerobic exercise such as running, swimming or dancing.

Frank Sinatra was the King of breathing! He could sing a remarkable number of lines in a row without stopping for breath and used this technique to enhance his performance. He used to increase his lung capacity by swimming under water. He would sing through the song in his head as he swam. It can really add to a performance when you are able to run lines into one another but it takes good breath control to achieve this. Equally, if your breath control is weak, it can intrude on the performance of a song. When a word has to be broken up in order to take a breath it loses its meaning. Try it out and you'll see.

Breathe in and say the whole line (with feeling), 'You left me and my heart is broken.' Now do the same (with feeling) but put a breath in the middle of the word 'broken'. Say, 'You left me and my heart is bro – ken.'

It sounds disjointed, doesn't it? You've lost all sense of the meaning of the sentence. The same goes for when you sing. Try to increase your lung capacity so that it carries you through to the end of the lines.

YES BUT: When I breathe in, my stomach goes in not out.

ANSWER: If you have a real problem locating where to breathe from, try lying on your back and feel what happens as you breathe normally. You will notice your tummy going up and down. This is the level of relaxation you need to achieve with your tummy muscles when you are standing.

INTRODUCING PLACEMENT

THE JOURNEY FROM BREATHING

So the air travels up from the lungs and the vocal cords are drawn together to make sound. The key to the sound you make is based on the *placement* you use. In other words, the different surfaces of the mouth and head give different sounds.

The soft palate – This is found by running your tongue along the roof of your mouth. About two thirds of the way back the roof of your mouth suddenly goes soft and jelly-like. This area is known as your 'soft palate'. If you aim the air to this area you will find the sound is dark and hollow. It is a soft surface so it will not give you bright sounds.

Forward placement – If we aim the air toward the front of the mouth think about the surfaces we are going to hit there: the bone of the cheeks, the cavities under the cheekbones, the gristly nose, and hard teeth. At the front of the face you have your very own sound chamber! Not only this, just look at the roof of the mouth. It's shaped like a chapel ceiling. As the air travels over this vaulted area the potential for different sounds is awesome.

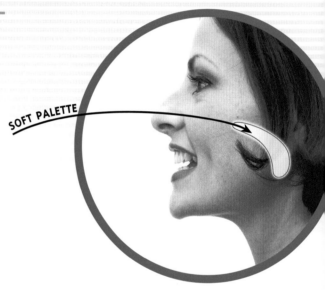

SOFT PALETTE

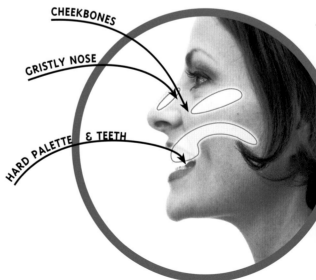

CHEEKBONES

GRISTLY NOSE

HARD PALETTE & TEETH

Singers who use only the soft palate all tend to have the same dark, hollow sound quality to their voices. The soft palate doesn't differ greatly from person to person. Now think about what the face and skull look like.

Everyone looks different and the surfaces at the front of the face have so much more individual variation allowing for the uniqueness of your sound to emerge. Not only this, but when you sing into a microphone, as we do in the music industry, it will pick up all the resonance that is achieved from forward placement. The quality of the sound will have brilliance to it, making your voice a lot more recordable.

Accents – The way you speak has a big influence on the way you sing. People who live in or come from cold countries tend to speak on the soft palate – think Margaret Thatcher or Princess Diana. The sound is further back in the throat. By way of contrast think of the accents that can be heard in hotter countries, such as those around the Mediterranean for instance. The 'mama mia' of Italy has a brighter sound placed much further forward in the mouth. This is where we encourage you to place your voice.

THE CHIN

With the artists we train we can tell almost immediately if they are used to performing in front of an audience. The tell tale sign is that those who have will normally push the chin forward of their body. This is probably something to do with their desire to reach the audience.

Many people raise their chins when they come to sing. Sometimes it's a performance style that makes the singer look passionate about what they are singing. Years of watching pop stars on TV with their chins in the air have led to this becoming the norm!

When the chin is raised this closes the gap at the back of the throat and the air is squeezed through the cords and on to the middle of the roof of the mouth. This gives a hard sound but it will sound increasingly more strangled as you go up in your range. On top of this it is also a far from safe way of singing.

THE JAW

We talked about the air being aimed towards the front of the mouth, and the potential of this 'forward placement', so now let's look at how the jaw is used to complete the sound system.

1. **Teeth together**

2. **Jaw forward**

3. **Jaw opened straight**

4. **Jaw pulled back**

If the jaws are locked together or the chin is pushed forward the sound will be contained within the mouth. By pulling the jaw back a gap is formed allowing full amplification of the sound. The air travelling over the roof of the mouth has a wider outlet and is not stifled in any way. The jaw should open backwards, loosely, like a trapdoor.

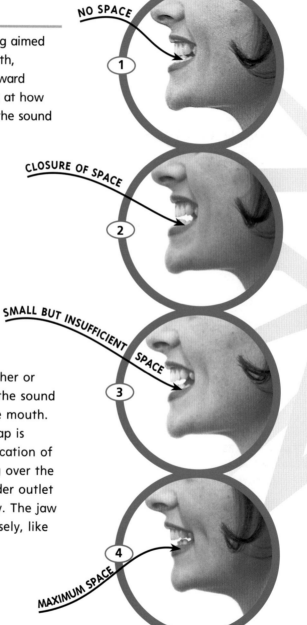

NO SPACE

1

CLOSURE OF SPACE

2

SMALL BUT INSUFFICIENT SPACE

3

4

MAXIMUM SPACE

HUMMING

Humming is where we begin once you have done your breathing exercises. As we saw in our medical pictures the vocal cords are folds of muscle and as such don't take well to sudden extreme action. It's like jumping out of bed in the morning and kicking your leg up past your head. The muscles in your leg would soon start telling you this was not a good idea! So it is with the vocal cords. Trying to hit top 'C' from cold is not advisable. A warm-up should start off gently and humming is the best kick-off point. When you begin to hum you should imagine that your voice wants to escape through your mouth and only the lips stand in its way. By the end of the exercise your lips should feel itchy with the vibration of the voice.

HUMMING EXERCISE

 CD EXERCISE I

The humming exercise should be a series of notes taking you up three to four intervals and back down again – the same as piano scales. Keep away from the extreme high and low notes in your range at this point and don't forget to breathe properly.

CD EXERCISE I ENDS

SPEAK-SINGING

After humming the next step is speak-singing. If a close friend of yours were speaking on the telephone how long would it take for you to recognise their voice? Probably a couple of sentences at most. In fact many of us would probably be able to identify a vast number of our friends and family through their spoken voices alone. Think about it: your voice has its own unique sound and if you sing and speak from the same place you should have lots of vocal identity.

The idea of the speak-singing exercise is that we don't hold the notes, we simply punch them out in a spoken style. Speaking and singing are closely connected. Every word we speak has a note, all we're doing in this exercise is choosing which note we go to. So think of it as speaking with a chosen note attached. This exercise can help people who really consider themselves as non-singers to sing. Don't do the exercise too loudly and the voice should glide up and down. Remember to inhale between each phrase and relax the lower abdominal muscles.

SPEAK-SINGING EXERCISE

We tend to use the same melody and note range as we used for the humming with a series of words like:

'I am learning how to sing'

'I am learning how to sing'

'That is why I am practising'

'That is what I am practising'

'I am learning as I go'

'I am learning as I go'

'Learning fast and learning slow'

'Learning fast and learning slow'

'I'm developing my range'

'I'm developing my range'

'Soon I'll start to hear a change'

'Soon I'll start to hear a change'

'I am singing low and high'

'I am singing low and high'

'Getting better as I try'

'Getting better as I try'

'I am learning everything'

'I am learning everything'

'Cos I really love to sing'

'Cos I really love to sing'

'I'm developing my range'

'I'm developing my range'

'Soon I'll start to hear a change'

'Soon I'll start to hear a change'

'When I'm singing at my best'

'When I'm singing at my best'

'Even I will be impressed'

'Even I will be impressed'

Try making up some of your own!

CD EXERCISE I ENDS

NASAL SINGING

Nasal singing is sometimes referred to as singing through the nose. Many singers today try to copy theatre or R'n'B singers and end up sounding very nasal (not like those they seek to imitate). It is strange that this sound is called singing through the nose because in fact that is exactly what is not happening.

When you sing like this you are blocking off the nose. Try singing and holding your nose and you'll see what we mean. It's a sound that makes sense when listened to in your own head but sounds thin and tuneless in the real world so try to steer clear of nasal singing. If you practise your speak-singing, keeping the placement at the front of the mouth and using your jaw properly (as directed previously) you should solve the problem.

YES BUT: I don't like the sound I'm making.

ANSWER: You don't have to sound like this when you sing songs but in order to get the voice warm a bright forward sound will "place" it correctly and give you the foundation for your "sound."

CHAPTER TEN

TUNING PROBLEMS

OVER THE YEARS the single most repeated problem singers have talked to us about is trying to stay in tune. It stops many people from enjoying their voices, even causing some to claim they are 'tone deaf'. If you've ever been to a Karaoke bar you will notice there are always a couple of people in every group who absolutely will not get up and sing. Sometimes it's a confidence issue but more often than not it's because they believe they cannot sing in tune.

YES BUT: I'm really tone deaf. Can I be taught to sing?

ANSWER: In our experience, most people who think they are tone deaf aren't at all. Either they haven't sung for years so are a bit rusty or they have some experience where someone has told them they can't sing. We've lost count of the number of people who were thrown out of their school choir or told to mime! That's a confidence issue. For most people it's about learning not to sing but to listen.

This leads us to the next most commonly asked question: 'Can you teach anyone to sing?' Well, so far the answer has been yes but normally the problem that most people face if they think they cannot sing is one of tuning. In reality we have never met anyone (so far) who is truly tone deaf. Maybe they exist out there but we have worked with thousands of professional and non-professional singers and, with some help, all of them could hold a tune.

Inaccurate tuning or pitching is a problem that almost every singer experiences at different times and for different reasons, but normally the root causes are the same. Bad placement or breathing are common causes and sometimes more complex problems can be due to a difficulty with listening. Temporary

tuning problems are sometimes caused by tiredness or ill health. Here are some pointers to help you with any tuning problems you may have.

PLACEMENT

When the air is aimed at the back of the throat, with its hollow soft-palate sound, it is more difficult to rein in and keep under control. It's like trying to stay on an untamed horse! Some people who have large-range voices find it hard to stay in tune in the middle section of their voice.

We are going to talk about this middle area later but be encouraged – big voices often take more time to learn how to control. If you have problems staying in tune try the placement teaching we talk about in the following chapters. This should help.

BREATHING

This is another reason for tuning problems. If you find the ends of your notes tend to stray off key or sound shaky it is usually because you are running out of breath. Remember to breath low, relaxing those tummy muscles.

It may seem a silly thing to mention but remember to breathe. Many singers have great lung capacity but they forget to breathe, trying to sing a number of lines in a row with no intake of breath. If you can get through many lines without stopping for breath and keeping your support that's great. If you can't, then breathe!

EAR TRAINING

This is all about learning to listen. Most singers are not great listeners as they are usually more interested in the sound of their own voice! Listening is one of the single most important things any musician or singer needs to master. Listening allows you both to achieve your potential and fully enjoy your music.

What most people need to learn are the intervals (the relationships) between notes and this is best helped by the use of a piano (or a melodic instrument). You don't need to be able to play. Strike any two notes that are quite close together – don't play chords, which comprise a number of different notes. Just two separate notes. Listen to the sound. Which one is higher and which one is lower? What is the relationship? Does it seem a lot higher/lower or only a little bit higher/lower? Try another two and ask yourself the same question. Don't just look at the notes, really listen to them.

Now try to add your voice. Play one note and then try to sing exactly that note. If it sounds wrong ask yourself, 'Am I singing higher than the note or am I singing lower than the note? Am I under (flat) or over (sharp) the note I am playing?'

Try to correct yourself as you do so. The problem is not that you sing the note out of tune, it is that you don't know how to correct it. Ear training is laborious but works wonders. If you can train yourself to listen to the notes properly you should be able to train your voice to follow your ears.

If you do not have access to a musical instrument go through the CD accompanying this book and simply try the first few exercises, concentrating on the tuning and really listening to the notes.

We have worked with artists who have fantastic voices with heaps of identity. Sometimes they will have no problem with tuning but have a problem with relative pitch. This means they can sing a melody completely in tune and yet be in a completely different key to the band (musical backing).

Over a number of weeks we will go through the painstaking task of playing a series of notes and then getting the artist to sing them back exactly. This helps to kick-start the ears into listening out for the notes.

CARRIE: I have been working with a great artist called Ashley Hamilton who has the most fantastic voice. It has heaps of identity. When I first started working with him he had no problems tuning but had a problem with relative pitch. This means he could sing a melody completely in tune and yet be in a completely different key from the band (musical backing).

Over a number of weeks we went through the painstaking task of playing a series of notes and then listening to him sing them back exactly. This kick-started his ears into listening to the notes and worked to amazing effect, transforming his set. His music rocks!

ILLNESS

This is another reason for tuning problems. Colds, ear-aches and so on can all block the ears and affect our ability to hear properly. Check out chapter three for help with colds. Altitude changes can also affect the ears, for instance when flying. If your ears are blocked they will not be doing their job properly. I always have sympathy for the artist who has flown across the Atlantic with all the time changes and altitude problems. Their ears are often affected for a couple of days. Tiredness makes your ears less effective, especially if you have been listening to music at loud levels or spending days with heavy background noise. Try to spend time in silence and also try to catch up on sleep – it's a great healer for the ears.

CHAPTER ELEVEN

DEFINING PLACEMENT

CHEST AND HEAD VOICE

The voice can be divided into two distinct areas: the chest voice, which is sometimes referred to as the 'full' voice, and the head voice, which is sometimes referred to as the falsetto voice. For the purposes of our teaching we will call them chest and head voices. The chest voice is the lower, fuller sounding voice from the bottom of your range to the upper middle and the head voice is the lighter sounding voice that takes you from the upper middle of your range to the top.

The breaking point –

Sometimes known as the bridge or *passaggio*, this is the part of the voice smack bang between your chest and your head voice, the bit in the middle that just about every singer struggles with. Some of us may struggle with one or two notes and others have big gaping holes in the middle of five or six notes.

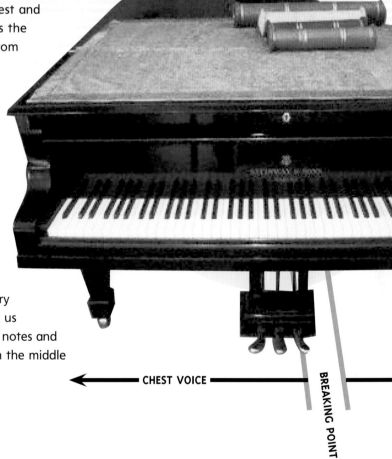

CHEST VOICE

BREAKING POINT

CHAPTER II

The problem – If you try to sing in your chest voice over the breaking point you may find the sound you produce is ugly, too loud and shouty and you may have to raise your chin to squeeze the notes out. If you cannot shout your way through the only alternative you have is to use your head voice, which is usually totally wimpy over the breaking point because it is too low.

Nearly every pop song ever written will cover this middle area of the voice and usually it is at the real belting part of the song. This is the part we call the 'money moment', the magical part that sells the record.

The solution – Forward placement allows you to cross between the chest and the head voice with one sound.

ONE VOICE

Many singers and just as many teachers are obsessed with developing the head and chest voices as separate entities. This teaching works from a technical point of view but is of limited use when it comes to singing modern songs. It's hard to sell a song with two completely different sounding voices. Some classical teaching in the UK counteracts this by teaching head voice only all the way up and down the range. This deals with the problem of having a sudden change in the two voices but the sound is usually aimed toward the forehead, giving a muffled tone which is powerless lower down in the range – not one we can use in modern pop music.

◀ HEAD VOICE ➡

The voice should sound like one powerful instrument, up and down, a seamless sound. We believe forward placement is the answer.

Think of the way the swan works. Above the surface the swan glides along giving no clues as to what is taking place below. Under the water its feet are working like mad. When we sing it should be the same. We know all the gear changes we have to make but to the listener the voice should sound seamless and effortless.

SUSTAINED NOTES

Sustained or held notes give us ample time to get the voice into the right place. As you aim the air forward toward the back of the front teeth you should hear a brightness emerging in the sound as the air travels over the roof of the mouth. 'E' is the easiest vowel to place. In our exercises we hold the note on the 'E' vowel and then crescendo (get louder). As we do so we turn the vowel into an 'OO' sound. If you are unsure of how to get the 'E' sound right say out loud, '*mama mia*' and listen to where you place the bright-sounding 'E' of '*mia*'. This is the place you need to aim your singing toward.

Air on your voice – By sustaining (holding) the note you can experiment until you get it right. You may find that to begin with the notes you sing are accompanied by lots of air. Try to take all the air off and make the voice completely pure when you are warming up. A breathy sound can be very useful as an additional effect but it is unsafe to push the cords together constantly in this way when singing. If you love the sound of the air on your voice and you see this as part of your identity that's fine, but as we said before, lay the foundations of forward placement and then add the effects.

CARRIE: When I first went to singing lessons I had loads of air on my voice. My teacher told me to imagine a candle in front of me as I sang. If the candle flame wavered I was using too much air. It had an amazing effect and I was able to take the air off almost immediately.

HOT TIP – If you have a problem with running out of breath when you sing you may find it is because you are wasting all the air on the sound of the note.

EXERCISE: SUSTAINED VOWELS

CD EXERCISE 3

Starting quietly on the 'E' vowel, after four beats turn it into an 'OO'. Crescendo (get louder) as you do so. Rather than seeing the exercise as two distinct vowels think of the latter vowel emerging from the former. The 'E' is transformed into whatever the next vowel is (like video morphing). Make sure your jaw/chin doesn't come out or up as you crescendo and don't forget to breathe!

1. *E to OO*
2. *E to OH*
3. *E to AH*
4. *E to EH*
5. *E to OR*

Some singers put a consonant at the beginning of vowel sounds. For instance, they will sing '**HEE OO**' and '**HEE AH**'. Not only does this sound a bit strange, you are also wasting lots of breath on the initial entry of the note and as a result may run out of breath by the end.

When you are singing '**OO**' keep your lips relaxed. Look in the mirror and say, 'True, two, who, you, new'. If you are speaking normally the chances are you are not funnelling your lips on the '**OO**' vowel sound.

It's a strange thing that when people sing they contort their lips forward. This can distort your forward placement so try to keep it as relaxed as you would when speaking.

As you go through the different vowel sounds you will find some easier to place than others. The 'OH' and 'AH' are particularly difficult as the air seems desperate to go up on to the soft palate, leaving you with a bright 'E' sound followed by a hollow 'AH'. Also, as the exercise travels up higher you will find it harder, especially across your breaking point. Try as hard as you can to keep the sound bright and forward at this point. If the sound is lifeless and wimpy you are probably using too much head voice and if the sound is shouty and uncontrollable you are probably using too much chest voice. Forward placement will come. Keep trying until you achieve it. If you imagine your voice has been set in its current position for your whole life and suddenly you are asking it to go somewhere else you will understand why it may not move in a hurry. Sometimes it can take a while to achieve this, perhaps even a number of weeks. Remember: it takes six weeks to break a habit.

The roof of the mouth is like a bridge. Imagine the sound having to travel forward over the bridge to the front of the mouth. Each time you hit the note you cross the bridge.

Diphthong – Make sure the vowels remain open as you sing. For instance do not put a hard 'W' on the end of 'OOH' or 'OH' vowels or a 'Y' on the end of 'EH'.

CD EXERCISE 3 ENDS

THE TONGUE

When singing, the tongue should be kept flat in order to make way for the air to get through. The tip of the tongue should rest on the back of the front, bottom teeth.

Key information can take a while to understand on both a mental and physical level. When you first learn to do anything, such as dancing or driving, there seems to be so much to take in and remember. You get one thing right and the focus on this area causes another area to be neglected. Over the weeks, as you continue to practise, you will find your co-ordination improves and after a while you will begin to think in your new technique. It won't occur to you to go back

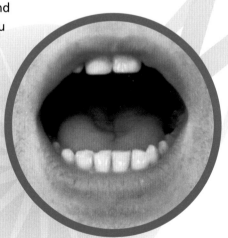

to the old way. When you learn a new language it is one thing to understand it, but it is quite another to think in that language. Singing technique is the same. The aim is to think in the new language.

> **HOT TIP** – If you find it hard to place the '**AH**' then put an '**EH**' in the middle of the exercise. For difficulty with '**OH**' put '**OO**' in the middle.

FOLLOW THROUGH

While you are mastering breathing and placement it's important that you begin to transfer this through to your song singing. There are plenty of students out there who have great technique in their exercises but have no idea how to make it through to the next stage. Think about a song you would like to sing. Think about the notes you find difficult. Remember when you come to sing full songs that they are a series of these forward-placed vowels. The technique applies to both the exercise and the song.

ADVANCED TECHNIQUE: Once you have established your forward placement across the break you can begin to do what's known as "mixing." This is where the head and the chest voice are used together. Low down in the break there will be more chest and a little head. Going through to the middle, half and half and as you rise to the top end of the break there will be less chest and more head voice. A good tip is to try singing in your chest voice but quietly (ie not with too much attach on the note).

```
                                    LOW ← HEAD → HIGH

        LOW ← CHEST → HIGH
```

YES BUT: No matter how much I try my voice sounds so weak when I'm at the top of my breaking point.

ANSWER: If you have pushed your chest voice it will take time for the head voice to get strong and bright. The cords are muscles remember so it takes time to build the strength in them and also to take them into a new place when you sing. If you can get the "E" vowel forward then eventually the others will follow.

CHAPTER TWELVE

DEVELOPING PLACEMENT

YOU CAN ESTABLISH forward placement on sustained notes when you have time to hear where the voice is currently placed and then respond by putting the voice into the correct place. Where the voice is at its weakest across the break (breaking point) it may not be easy to achieve instantly so every note on each of the sustained exercises has to be worked through slowly and, if necessary, repeated.

Following on from this the next step is to take that forward placement and see if you can achieve it on shorter, more clipped notes, hitting the placement in an instant with no time to hear and therefore develop the sound. The voice has to go to the right placement from memory.

EXERCISE: MAMA MIA FETTUCCINE

 **CD EXERCISE 4**

We use the words 'mama mia fettuccine' because the Italian accent is so beautifully placed at the front of the face. Imagine you are in Rome and you have been offered the greatest bowl of pasta ever (if you don't like pasta then you'll have to act this one). Your response is to sing 'mama mia fettuccine'. Sing with real passion!

It may feel embarrassing but it's a great exercise. The top notes must sound strong. If you try chesting them you will be shouting and doing your vocal chords damage. If you sing them completely in your head voice they will sound weak and like 'cod-opera'! Forward placement will give you the brightness you need. It should sound as strong as a chest voice but have a real ease of performance.

CD EXERCISE 4 ENDS

> **HOT TIP** – Don't start the exercise by singing too loudly or you will find when you get to the middle of your range, it will be like diving off a cliff into wimpsville!

SWAN TACTICS

As the exercise travels up in your range so your break will come at different parts of the melody. This will make your voice sound lumpy and disjointed until you have learned to change gears smoothly from chest across the break into head and back down again. By placing the whole voice forward you should, with practise, be able to cross smoothly.

Remember the swan analogy. Especially watch out for the last syllable, 'ni'. Most people are so pleased at having achieved the top note they completely neglect placing the final note.

VOWEL SOUNDS

All great singers distort the vowels to work in their favour. By this we mean the following: Say for instance, you decide to sing 'macaroni' instead of 'fettucine', on the 'macaroni' you may struggle to hit the top note with forward placement because it's that nasty 'OH' vowel we came across during the sustained note section. Try changing the 'OH' vowel to an 'AH' vowel, so it becomes 'maca RAH ni'. You will probably find it a lot easier.

Aretha Franklin has great forward placement. She also completely distorts her vowels to suit the sound, especially high up in her range. So 'LOVE' becomes 'LAV' and 'BEFORE' becomes 'BEFAR'. Another singer who applies vowel distortion is Anastacia. Try it out on your own songs and you'll see them transformed.

GLOTTAL ATTACK

One of the primary causes of nodules is the over use of the glottal attack (or onset, as it is sometimes called). What we do when we 'glottal' is bang the vocal cords together harshly to form a word or note. Can you imagine doing this night after night over a number of years? Eventually, in order to cope with being constantly banged together, hard spots develop, corresponding on either side of the chords. These spots are called nodules. Glottal attack happens particularly with words starting with a vowel. We hit the vowel from the throat, in a hard way, to give power and volume and yet the impetus for the power and volume should come from the stomach muscles, supporting the diaphragm as it forces the breath out. The 'cut' or 'edge' of a note should be made low down in the body, not in the throat.

David and I have a doubly hard time because we have both grown up in London where glottal attack is in constant use in our speech. When we say the name 'Pete', for instance, we never get the 'T' of Pete into the mouth; we form it down in the throat.

YES BUT: I'm managing to get the top note bright, but then the last lower note sounds really weak.

ANSWER: As you get higher, the top note will be in your head range but the last note still in your chest so it's important to remember to change back down to chest. It's quite a big jump but this represents the kind of interval jumps you would be expected to sing in songs.

EXERCISE: GLOTTAL ATTACK

CD EXERCISE 5

We use the same melody as our sustained note exercise but now with one beat for each note down. We go through different vowel sounds as we go.

Breathe between each note and try a crescendo on the fourth note each time. You may find it hard to crescendo some vowels but keep it up and you should begin to see a difference. As you put power behind each note you should be able to see your abdomen going in and out.

1. *EE, EE, EE, EE*
2. *OO, OO, OO, OO*
3. *OH, OH, OH, OH*
4. *AY, AY, AY, AY*
5. *EYE, EYE, EYE, EYE*
6. *OR, OR, OR, OR*
7. *AH, AH, AH, AH*

CHECKLIST: Don't forget to breathe properly, take the air off, keep the placement forward, and don't put an 'H' sound on the front of the vowels.

CD EXERCISE 5 ENDS

CHAPTER THIRTEEN

INCREASING YOUR RANGE

It's amazing to hear singers talk about the things they think they cannot do. Some singers come fully loaded with all sorts of restrictions they have placed on their voices. One of the most popular ones we hear when people come for a session with us is either 'I don't sing low' or, more often, 'I don't sing high'.

Singers are afraid of the extremities of the voice, preferring to stay in the safe places rather than venturing out. Expanding your vocal range is a great thing to do, but remember, most songs do not have more than one and a half octave ranges in them (that's eighteen notes including all the semitones or half-notes). Also remember it's not a competition to see who has the most notes in their range. Singing is an art not a sport! Most singers can manage two to three octaves but this can vary from one to four and a half. It's not about how many notes you have, it's what you do with them that counts.

It is said that Billie Holiday only ever had a one-octave range. Just think: a whole career built on just twelve notes. The quality of the sound of those twelve notes and the soulfulness with which she performed was awesome. She made every note count.

BAND MENTALITY

When people work together, singing in groups, each singer tends to claim their piece of land and sticks to it. We have found this is the case with all the pop bands we have coached. From Take That through to The Spice Girls, from S Club to Atomic Kitten, each singer has tended to state what they are good at and be unable to believe they can do anything else. 'I'm the low singer.' 'I'm the high singer.' 'I'm the song-writer.' 'I'm the dancer.'

When we first worked with Take That (the first time round) each member had a distinct role. Jason and Howard were the dancers, Robbie and Mark were the teen heart-throbs and Gary was the singer/songwriter. Robbie was incredibly talented (as has since been proven) but in this situation there was never room for him to shine fully.

Having different roles is helpful in a band setting but very unhelpful when it comes to developing your own voice and performance fully. Many of those so-called low singers have great high ranges that had gone undiscovered until they came for coaching.

SINGING TYPE

Singers can be defined by their different voice types. Voice types starting at the bottom go as follows:

BASS:	VERY LOW male voice
BARITONE:	MID/LOW male voice
TENOR:	HIGH/MID male voice
HIGH TENOR:	HIGH male voice (sometime called counter tenor)
TREBLE:	Boy's voice
CONTRALTO:	LOW female voice
ALTO:	MID/LOW female voice
MEZZO/SOPRANO:	MID/HIGH female voice
SOPRANO:	HIGH female voice

The range you have doesn't necessarily dictate what singing type you are. We like to define the singing type by where the voice is at its richest and most resonant, where it jumps out and comes alive. If, for instance, you define yourself as a soprano this does not mean you will never sing or will be unable to sing low down in your range.

The castrati – Derived from Italy, these were young boys between the ages of 8 and 10 who were literally castrated in order to keep their voices sounding young. They were viewed as precious spectacles. The practice has been outlawed and the last of them died in the early twentieth century.

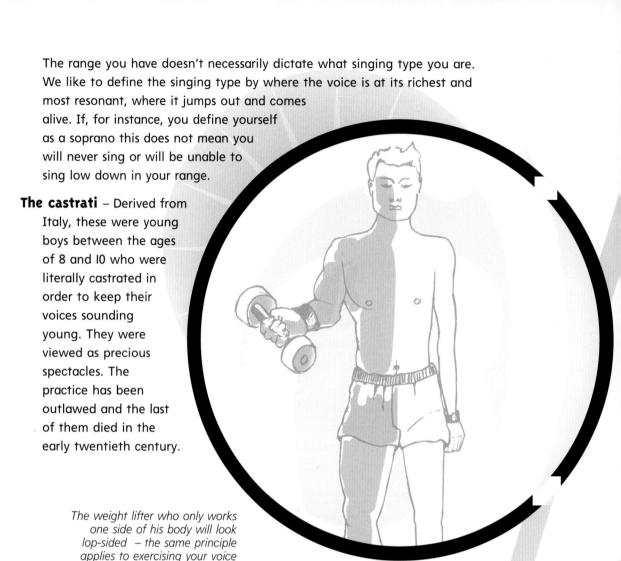

The weight lifter who only works one side of his body will look lop-sided – the same principle applies to exercising your voice

KEEPING BALANCE

It's important to keep a balance in the training of your voice. If you work only one end you will probably find the other end becomes weakened and vice versa. People who use only their chest voices tend to have incredibly weak head voices and people who use only their head voices tend to struggle even to find a chest voice. The neglected area sounds out of control. It's a bit like weight lifting.

In modern music, if the voice is trained unevenly you will find it hard to sing complete repertoires. Try to work the areas of your voice that are weak rather than sticking with what already sounds good. The potential for a bigger voice is there, but it's down to you to discover it.

EXERCISE: RANGE UP

 CD EXERCISE 6

As you sing the exercise remember to keep your placement. The words are:

1. Have a wonderful day
2. Have a marvellous day
3. Have a beautiful day

As you get to the top of your range don't pull back or step back, be committed to hitting those high notes. Remember the impetus for reaching the top notes comes from the breath you are powerfully kicking out with your stomach muscles, supporting the diaphragm. Check yourself in the mirror to make sure you are not raising or pushing your chin out. If anything pull the chin back the higher you go. The face should remain completely relaxed, no grimacing. Don't raise the corners of your mouth or eyebrows. Let the voice do the communicating. When you sing the high notes try not to think of reaching up for them but gliding over them.

Lifting – To help you achieve your high notes try lifting the windowsill (or any other immoveable object at around waist height). Stand facing the window with your knees slightly bent, feet parallel. Completely relax your tummy muscles as you breathe in. Keeping your knees bent, try to lift the windowsill (make sure it's secure!) and as you

This exercise will help you achieve your high notes

do so check what happens to your tummy muscles. They should tighten. These are the same muscles that you use to support your breathing when singing.

Previously difficult notes can be kicked out with this sudden power from the lower abdominals. Now try it on the exercise. Do exactly what we have listed above and as you get to the high notes lift the windowsill. Remember to breathe properly between each line. When you've managed to achieve the notes by lifting try the exercise again, using the same muscles but without lifting.

Folding – Sometimes high notes are hard to reach because often we think we cannot reach up for them. Try folding yourself over to 90° each time you have to hit the high note and you will be amazed at how the air is forced out.

Bending – If you are struggling with the high range another tip we sometimes use is to bend the knees slightly as we sing top notes. In a way it is like a combination of the windowsill and folding advice given. It reminds us to breath low and support and it takes us away from the fear as we physically move in the opposite direction to the note.

CD EXERCISE 6 ENDS

EXERCISE: RANGE DOWN

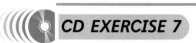 *CD EXERCISE 7*

The next exercise takes us down in the range. As you cross your breaking point don't stay in your head voice but reach for the fuller chest voice as you get down low. Always remember to keep your forward placement!

It is just as important to support the voice when you are singing low as high. The lower you sing the more air is used so don't forget to breathe properly. Don't let the sound get too dark. Keep it bright and try to keep your forward placement from the top to the bottom.

We do this exercise on 'E' vowel.

Most people think of Karen Carpenter and Nat King Cole as having low voices but in fact they simply used richer, darker tones to give a low effect. Check out the 'Paint Palette' section for more details.

CD EXERCISE 7 ENDS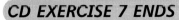

EXERCISE — OCTAVE JUMPS

 CD EXERCISE 8

This exercise takes you both up and down in your range. We hit the bottom note then jump to the octave above and then come back down again. Try each complete octave jump (the three notes down, up and back down again) on one vowel sound and then change for the next set.

① *'AY'*　③ *'EE'*　⑤ *'AH'*　⑦ *'I'*

② *'OO'*　④ *'OH'*　⑥ *'OR'*　⑧ *'EH'*

Go back to the top when you have completed all eight sounds. Remember to breathe properly and make sure you keep a consistent tone through forward placement.

ADVANCED TECHNIQUE - TONAL BREAKS

Most people, once they've established a smooth way through the breaking point, begin to notice what we can "tonal breaks." These can be described as a change in the sound or tone of the voice a few notes either side of your break. They are like "mini" breaking points and need to be navigated so that there isn't a sudden change in tone. They are not so hard to work through as the breaking point itself (often the singer will have the power to get the note out) but it's important to make sure the tone is consistent.

YES BUT: I used to be able to hit really low/high notes and I seem to have lost that ability.

ANSWER: There are so many reasons why a singer loses range: it could be tiredness or the vocal cords developing and changing with age, but more often than not it is because the songs they have been singing are in a particular range of the voice, and the other end of the vocal range gets neglected. That's why warming up the whole voice is important.

CD EXERCISE 8 ENDS

CHAPTER FOURTEEN

THE PAINT PALETTE

THERE IS NOTHING MORE BEAUTIFUL than listening to a singer who is totally in control of his or her voice. They can use the voice to convey any emotion they desire.

A singer who has control over their voice will be able to use different textures and tones, light and shade, breathiness and purity. During our next set of exercises we are going to experiment with a few different colours and styles.

One of the most important things to remember when singing is that *breath informs tone*. We talk a lot about the placement of the voice bringing the sound, but the amount of air being released is just as important. That is why supporting the voice with the breathing technique we have shown you is vital. Once we start to play around with the sound of the voice, having as much air as possible to release or hold back will have a huge impact on the sound you are able to achieve.

DARKER TONES

This is where we begin to reintroduce some of the hollow sounds achieved at the back of the throat. This is not to say we completely neglect forward placement, but the darker sound is simply *added* to the bright front sound.

You achieve this by singing with forward placement but lowering the back of the tongue, as though yawning. This opens up the back of the throat, giving a richer, darker tone. Remember the weight lifter – you must build up the strength in the forward placement before reintroducing other tones.

DARK TONE EXERCISE

 CD EXERCISE 9

AFTER you have established forward placement (so not in the first few lessons) we suggest you use the 'Range Down' exercise to establish this darker sound. Think of

approaching the note from underneath to get the darker sound. Play around with the sound until you find one that doesn't sound either too dark or too light.

CD EXERCISE 9 ENDS

CRESCENDO/DIMINUENDO

One of the tell-tale signs of a good singer is their ability to both crescendo (get louder) and diminuendo (get quieter). If you sing too high in your chest voice you will not be able to get quieter on the notes. You will either stop dead and have a heavy glottal sound on the end or you'll riff off them. With forward placement you should be able to get louder or quieter with ease and control.

CRESCENDO/DIMINUENDO EXERCISE

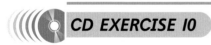

CD EXERCISE 10

Sing the following series of words and crescendo and diminuendo as you reach the final note. Try to do each phrase in one breath.

1. *When people hear*
2. *A voice they love*
3. *It makes them feel*
4. *Deep in their soul*

1. *As though the one*
2. *Who has the voice*
3. *Sings just for them*
4. *And them alone*

CD EXERCISE 10 ENDS

VIBRATO

Vibrato (or vib) is the oscillation between two notes. It is the vibration or shaky undulation of the voice. Some people have lots of vibrato on their voice and others none. Some schools of thought believe that you cannot create vibrato, that it is something you naturally have or don't have on your voice but we have seen many students develop their vibrato. When you learn to control your vibrato you should be able to put it on or take it off the notes and give different speeds of vibrato.

VIBRATO EXERCISE

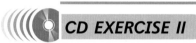 **CD EXERCISE II**

The exercise is the same as the 'Crescendo/Diminuendo' exercise. This time don't crescendo or diminuendo but try the following on the ends of the phrase:

1	*When people hear*	NO VIB AT ALL
2	*A voice they love*	SLOW VIB
3	*It makes them feel*	FAST VIB
4	*Deep in their soul*	NONE TO FAST VIB
5	*As though the one*	SLOW TO NO VIB
6	*Who has the voice*	FAST TO SLOW VIB
7	*Sings just for them*	NO TO SLOW TO FAST TO NO VIB
8	*And them alone*	ANY COMBINATION YOU LIKE!

 **CD EXERCISE II ENDS**

LIGHT AND SHADE

It's really important to remember that singing should have light and shade. We will talk more about this in the 'How To Vocally Interpret a Song' chapter but even in our exercises we can begin to develop the ability to sing both loudly and quietly. The voice should have both power and gentleness.

LIGHT AND SHADE EXERCISE

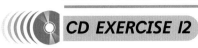

CD EXERCISE 12

The words of the exercise are 'You're wonderful, you're beautiful'. We are going to sing the 'You're wonderful...' part loudly and the '...you're beautiful' part quietly. The idea is that you keep forward placement for both. One should not sound loud and clear and the other breathy. Both should sound the same but as though someone has literally turned the volume down. When you get this it should sound beautiful. It may help you to think of the volume changes as a parent and a child. The parent, strong and assured; the child, quieter and more vulnerable.

Loudly	Quietly
'YOU'RE WONDERFUL...'	*'...YOU'RE BEAUTIFUL'*
'YOU'RE WONDERFUL...'	*'...YOU'RE BEAUTIFUL'*
'YOU'RE WONDERFUL...'	*'...YOU'RE BEAUTIFUL'*
'YOU'RE WONDERFUL...'	*'...YOU'RE BEAUTIFUL'*

CD EXERCISE 12 ENDS

FLEXIBILTY

Flexibility is the speed at which you can go from one note to the next. It is important to develop flexibility throughout the whole range with a whole series of notes. Good breathing is essential.

FLEXIBILITY EXERCISE

CD EXERCISE 13

The next exercise takes us all the way down in the range and then all the way back up. You need to take a big breath and hold the note for four counts on the end. On the way up we will say one word and on the way back down we will say another. Try to take one breath all the way down and another for the journey back down.

Downward	Upward
'I'	*'LOVE'*
'IT'	*'WHEN'*
'YOU'	*'SAY'*
'YOU'	*'LIKE'*
'MY'	*'VOICE'*
'IT'	*'MAKES'*
'ME'	*'FEEL'*
'MY'	*'WORK'*
'IS'	*'DONE'*

CD EXERCISE 13 ENDS

RIFFING

Also known as ad libbing or improvisation, riffing is where the singer goes away from the normal melody in order to create his or her own 'made up' melody. It can involve new words or simply be a series of 'oohs' or 'aahs'. You can have fast, intricate riffs or simply held notes. Anything goes! It's great to practise by taking any song or piece of music and singing your own thing over the top. After a while you'll really begin to enjoy it.

Remember that intricate riffing is only a series of notes sung quickly. Don't be intimidated. Start with sustained notes and work your way on to the more complex stuff. Developing your vibrato will help when it comes to riffing.

Stevie Wonder inspired many young artists today to use riffing in their music. His style and his ability to know where to – and not to – riff is impeccable. He never shows off and you never feel riffs are put in a song for the sake of it. He makes every one of them count.

Scat singing – This is where you sing 'be bop doo wap' type lyrics over the music. Used in jazz music particularly, it is a close relative of riffing. Experimentation should always take place in the 'safe space' – your car, bedroom, sitting room or rehearsal room. When it comes to riffing on stage you must have a few ad-libs up your sleeve to fall back on if all inspiration fails. Many singers wait until they are on stage in front of an audience to experiment. This is not a good idea. You would be amazed how much practise it takes to sound as though you're making it up as you go along! Some singers riff too much. Riffing should be used to sell the song not to show off. As we've said before, singing is an art not a sport! Don't become a riffamaniac! If you are using a vowel sound on an intricate, fast riff don't put consonants on the fronts of all the notes. Once or twice is fine.

RIFFING EXERCISE

CD EXERCISE 14

Using the 'You're wonderful, you're beautiful' pattern we are going to forget the loud/soft approach. Keeping it all at the same level we are now going to change the melody. We suggest you run the exercise through three times, developing your riffing as you do so.

(1) Keep the words. Riff anywhere you like. Take your riffs upward and downward.

(2) Now riff on the following words of the phrase:

Phrase No 1: Riff on 'WON'   **Phrase No 2:** Riff on 'YOU'RE'

Phrase No 3: Riff on 'FUL'   **Phrase No 4:** Riff on 'FUL'

Phrase No 5: Riff on 'WON'   **Phrase No 6:** Riff on 'YOU'RE'

Phrase No 7: Riff on 'FUL'   **Phrase No 8:** Riff on 'FUL'

Now take away all the words and phrasing and intricately riff trying to find all the unusual notes. It should sound very jazzy. In summary, if you master the shade, tones and skills of singing, when you come to sing full songs the choices and approaches you have will be so much greater.

CARRIE: I recently prepared Gwyneth Paltrow for a country movie she was working on. She had to sing country style so for the exercises in this section of the lesson she would be encouraged to move towards a more country sound, looking at tone, vowel sounds etc.

YES BUT: I listen to 'so-and-so' sing and I just can't get that fullness or fatness to the sound like they have. Is that because they are born with that sound?

ANSWER: Of course there's the obvious, 'don't compare yourself' answer, but beyond this there are a couple of things that have a huge impact on the voice. Firstly, the music you listen to has a profound impact on how you sing. If you grow up listening to R'n'B riffers the chances are you'll be able to riff yourself.

CD EXERCISE 14 ENDS

CHAPTER FIFTEEN

HOW TO INTERPRET A SONG VOCALLY

'A great singer is a song's best friend' – Quincy Jones

MANY SINGERS DEVELOP a thorough singing technique and yet they have no idea how to interpret a song. Every song tells a story. As a singer you share the story through your voice. The listener should be able to understand the story without seeing your face. The voice alone should communicate. When working on *talent shows* we have been amazed by how many people would choose a song (maybe one they've been singing for years) and have no idea what it was about. If you don't understand the lyric your listener will have no hope of understanding it either.

For example, on *Pop Idol* we had a singer who wanted to sing 'The Greatest Love Of All'. They thought the song was about parents loving their children when in fact it is about us learning to love ourselves. Another wanted to sing 'From This Moment On'. They thought it was about going out on your first date when in fact it is a wedding song!

Many singers do not think fully about the lyrics of their songs because they are preoccupied with the sound their voice is making – they become obsessed by notes. Sometimes it can be helpful to forget you are a singer and think of yourself as an actor or narrator instead.

GEAR CHANGING

Every song should have a beginning, a middle and an end. It should go through a number of vocal and emotional gear changes. If you only give your listener

15

top gear they'll get bored by the second verse. If you wait to give your top gear it will be amazing. It's all about the song having light and shade. Light can be shown as truly brilliant when it is set on a backdrop of darkness. Learn where the gear changes go up and down, where the song is relaxed and where it is intense. Don't feel you have to show everything you can do in the first couple of lines of a song. Delayed gratification can be immensely satisfying for your audience!

A good example of gear changing can be found in most modern pop ballads. They tend to go through a whole cycle, starting very low key, building up, peaking and then going back to the gear they first started in.

There are two ways to help you interpret songs.

EMOTIONAL

The first method is to see your performance as emotional. This is the more holistic approach. Rather than taking the song apart bit by bit ask yourself, 'What is the emotion of the song?' If you tell the story and allow the emotion to come through the words you will find you are naturally able to interpret the song. We have seen countless numbers of singers able to hit notes they thought they never could simply by letting go of the thought of singing and instead telling the story with their voices.

A technique we sometimes use to help singers interpret their songs is one where we ask questions between the lines as they sing. All they have to do is respond to the questions with the lyric of the song. For example, take the lyric to 'The Greatest Love Of All'. Imagine these questions being asked in the gaps as the song is being sung. (We have also written possible gear changes you may wish to follow.)

THE GREATEST LOVE OF ALL

QUESTION	LYRIC	GEAR
What do you believe?	*I believe that children are our future*	I
What should we do?	*Teach them well and let them lead the way*	
How?	*Show them all the beauty they possess inside*	
What else should we do?	*Give them a sense of pride*	
Why?	*To make it easier*	
What else?	*Let the children's laughter*	
Do what?	*Remind us how we used to be*	
What did you do?	*I decided long ago*	2
To do what?	*Never to walk in anyone's shadow*	
And?	*If I fail, if I succeed*	
What will you do?	*At least I've lived, as I believe*	
How do you feel?	*No matter what they take from me*	
What can't they do?	*They can't take away my dignity*	
Why?	*Because the greatest love of all*	3
Is doing what?	*Is happening to me*	
What have you found?	*I've found the greatest love of all*	
Where?	*Inside of me*	
What is it?	*The greatest love of all*	4
Is what?	*Is easy to achieve*	
Why?	*Learning to love yourself*	
Is what?	*Is the greatest love of all*	
What else?	*And if by chance that special place*	I
That what?	*That you've been dreaming of*	
Does what?	*Leads you to a lonely place*	
What should I do?	*Find your strength in love*	4

TECHNICAL

The second method is technical, taking the song apart note by note and word by word. Working out what sound would work for a particular word. For instance, if the word is 'softly' then sing softly. Going through some of the paint palette teaching (riffing, crescendo, diminuendo, etc) you can apply certain skills to match certain words and this will help you to create the overall performance.

WHINING AND GROANING

You may be saying to yourself, 'Surely I don't have to do that', but groaning on the front of a word or whining through certain words can be immensely powerful. Try it!

PRONUNCIATION

Some words close the mouth and shut off the sound too soon. For instance, on a word like 'SAY' or 'DAY' the 'Y' closes the jaw. Try to rewrite these words as 'SET' and 'DET'. With silent 'T's the note should sound much more powerful. When the end of a sustained note lands on a consonant try to leave the consonant off until the last possible moment. For instance, on the word 'Home' sing the 'OH' sound for as long as you can or you will be left singing the 'M' with very little opportunity for sound projection. It's worth taking a look at the lyrics of the songs before you come to sing them and going through any words where the vowels would be more powerful if changed.

Another little gospel trick is, when a long note ends in a 'T', leaving the 'T' to the last possible moment and then singing it with real clarity on the end.

Diphthong – A diphthong is where two vowels are joined together in a word and the sound of the second vowel follows closely behind the first. For example, the letters 'a' and 'i' form the diphthong in 'rain' (when singing check to see if your pronunciation becomes 'Ray – in'). Sometimes you may want to emphasise a diphthong and at other times it may suit the phrase to de-emphasise it. Look through your lyrics and check them out.

BREATHING

One thing that tends to happen when we come to sing songs is that we take a huge breath at the beginning of the introduction of the music in preparation for singing and then hold the breath, waiting for the lyric to come in. The best thing to do – and the way to take the biggest breath possible – is to exhale completely just before you sing. It is amazing how quickly you will take a deep breath just before the lyric comes in.

Some phrases in a song will suit not taking a breath in between so lines are carried over. This can be particularly effective if you have a big middle section to the song which then goes into the end chorus. Carrying over the breath can increase impact. Equally important, as we mentioned in the breathing section, is to try not to breathe in the middle of the word or it may lose its meaning.

Remember that if you have big high notes in the song your abdominal support is essential. Try the windowsill exercise we wrote about in the range chapter to help you with high or sustained notes.

Breathy tone – A breathy tone can be a great sound to have in your armoury. Try not to sing with breath on the notes all the time as it is not good for the voice, but used sparingly it can really add to a song. Use on the ends of lines or on certain words whose meaning fits the tone, etc.

Ends of lines – Many singers dip the volume on the ends of the lines. Try not to do this unless it really works for the lyric. Keeping the volume up at the end of lines can instantly make the voice sound fifty per cent stronger.

Placement jumping – Many singers use this technique in their songs. This is where a lower note is hit fairly loudly in the chest voice and then instantly followed by a gentle head note sound. Mariah Carey, Taylor Swift, Bono and many country and rock singers use this technique all the time. The interval between the notes varies but is usually a fifth (five scale notes up) and occasionally a whole octave.

CARRIE: When Shania Twain and Mariah Carey visited Fame Academy I was so encouraged to see their passion for singing. They were also both a little nervous, which made them even more appealing. Both have huge but very different voices and both really know how to tell the story of the song they are singing.

RIFFING

The technique of riffing is explained in the previous chapter. When riffing, by all means go away from the melody but don't forget to come back to it or the listener will lose their way and you will cease to communicate. If you are riffing over choruses make sure you have established the melody first. Remember, your listener loves to sing along but they won't be able to if you have not first let them know what the melody is.

Riffing and ad libbing covers a whole host of different techniques. Here are a few:

Sustained note riffing – This is where a singer uses a note to soar over the music. It can be with a word or a particular vowel.

Call and response – In true gospel style, this is where the singer either:

1   Repeats the line after the backing vocals have sung it; or

2   Announces the line before it has been sung.

Many singers are comfortable responding to lines but have never thought about announcing the line to come. For example, on a phrase like 'The greatest love of all is happening to me' the response ad lib could be 'The greatest love of all (LOVE OF ALL) is happening to me'. Whereas the call ad lib could be 'The greatest love of all (IS HAPPENING TO ME) is happening to me'.

Call ad libs can be really powerful and give the singer a real air of authority. With interpretation the ideal is for you to have a mixture of emotional and technical skills. With the combination of the two you should find your songs really take off.

YES BUT: How come I can hit the high note in one part of the song and yet struggle when it comes to that very same note later in the song?

ANSWER: This is because of the vowel sound. Some vowels are easier to sing. This is why the sustained vowels exercise is so important to master. An alternative way to approach the note is to distort the vowel. For example, it's rare to hear Aretha Franklin sing "love" with an "aah" vowel. It is more likely she'll distort the vowel to an "err" sound. "Err" is much easier to place forward.

CHAPTER SIXTEEN

HOW TO INTERPRET A SONG VISUALLY

No wrongs – We like to tell people there are no wrongs when it comes to how you want to perform. There are styles that are more acceptable for different types of music but it's great to let the barriers down and just let what's inside come out!

Improvement – An artist should never come to the stage with the attitude that they cannot improve upon their performance. There is always potential for growth and we should analyse our performance to see what has become stale and what needs to change. If you are bored with doing 'the same old thing' so will your audience be!

Vulnerability – Allowing yourself to be seen as vulnerable is a very powerful weapon in your performance armoury. We are vulnerable when we sing and often a singer feels as though they are baring their very soul. When you allow others in to observe your vulnerability it can be deeply moving.

Mirror – Before you get started a full-length mirror is a great tool to have. In front of the mirror you can learn what your body and face look like at every angle. If, when you are practising, you do something you like the look of you can mentally store it away for the performance later.

Eyes – It is said that the eyes are the window to the soul. Practise keeping your eyes open when performing. A performance where the artist keeps his or her eyes completely closed throughout feels like a very closed performance. The audience need to be 'let in' – and they 'get in' through the eyes. The odd moment or phrase with the eyes shut is not a problem. If it fits the song that's OK but if you close your eyes because you feel self-conscious that's not OK. It's something you can discipline yourself to do even if at first it seems difficult.

Eye contact – Never make prolonged eye contact with a member of the audience. It will unnerve them! Equally, no contact at all speaks of fear. Some eye contact is essential, but keep it natural.

Blinking – A bad habit that a lot of performers have is blinking in rhythm with the music or words. You often see TV presenters do this too, blinking to emphasise certain parts of the sentence. Check yourself on this one! Practise blinking slowly too as this can have great impact.

Stillness – Stillness is one of the most powerful tools a performer can use. Don't feel you have to throw in every trick like a circus performer. Stillness can convey emotion when you simply feel the lyrics of a song.

CARRIE: I remember when I was 16 years old performing in a show and Andrew Lloyd Webber came to see it. I was desperate to impress. Later the cast asked him what he looked for in a performance and he said, 'Stillness'. I suddenly realised I had a lot to learn. Allowing the inner emotion to speak is a great thing to master.

Hands – It's very hard to know what to do with one's hands. The more you concentrate on what to do with them the more ungainly they feel! If you have given yourself, or been given, specific moves to do, that's fine, but if you want to leave your hands relaxed at your sides, be aware that's fine too. It's a weird thing but if you are uncomfortable with your hands the audience will notice and, equally, if you are comfortable with them hanging at your sides then the audience in turn will feel your ease. It follows on from the stillness teaching – don't feel you have to be moving at all times.

PERFORMANCE MODES

There are three basic modes for your singing performance. Think of them as performance bubbles. You may use only one of them, or any combination of them, in order to enhance your performance.

Mode 1 – one to no one – This mode has the singer completely isolated and reflective. Imagine you are performing and no one is watching. You are totally in your own world. Even if there are people in front of you and you are looking toward them you do not come out of your own, isolated 'bubble'.

Mode 2 – one to one – This is the mode of performance where you are singing to one other person. Imagine you are singing and there is just one person you are singing to and about. Even if there are others in front of you, only one is allowed in your bubble. For TV performances this other person may be straight down the lens.

Mode 3 – one to many – This is the mode of performance where you are singing to many people at one time. Imagine a huge audience in front of you and you wanting to include them all in your communication.

Let's take a song and look at what possible modes of performance you might like to use.

THE GREATEST LOVE OF ALL

LYRIC	MODE
I believe that children are our future	2
Teach them well and let them lead the way	
Show them all the beauty they possess inside	
Give them a sense of pride to make it easier	
Let the children's laughter	
Remind us how we used to be	
I decide long ago never to walk in anyone's shadow	1
If I fail, if I succeed at least I've lived as I believe	
No matter what they take from me	
They can't take away my dignity	2
Because the greatest love of all is happening to me	3
I've found the greatest love of all inside of me	
The greatest love of all is easy to achieve	
Learning to love yourself	
Is the greatest love of all	
And if by chance that special place	2
That you've been dreaming of	
Leads you to a lonely place	1
Find your strength in love	3

These are rough suggestions. There are no hard and fast rules about what mode you should or shouldn't perform in. It's all down to how you feel you can best perform and communicate the song.

You may find you are already using these performance bubbles but no one has ever given you the language to express verbally what it is you are doing. Knowing how your performance can be broken down technically can be extremely helpful if you are ever struggling with the physical interpretation of a song.

Never forget that a good technically executed performance will never match a performance that has real emotion in it. Technicalities are there to enhance and assist your interpretation skills. They help you communicate emotion, but they are not a substitute for emotion.

RECOVERY

Learning how to recover when things go wrong is a skill in itself. Your face lets us know when you have made a mistake or if you are disappointed with your performance. Try to remember your audience often have no idea where you have gone wrong – you alone know how it is meant to be.

There is a wonderful story about Judy Garland playing the London Palladium. The concert was just starting and the band had struck up the music to 'Somewhere Over The Rainbow'. Judy Garland made her entrance on to the stage but lost her footing. As we all do in these situations she reached out for the nearest object to break her fall. Unfortunately for her, the only thing in front of her was the microphone stand, which of course was not fixed to the floor. She grabbed it and then, to everyone's horror, both she and the microphone went flying across the stage. So how do you recover from that? Well, Judy simply stayed on the floor, pulled the microphone to her and lying there began, 'Somewhere Over The Rainbow'! She received a standing ovation. Judy was so impressed she included the fall in every show after that!

CHAPTER SEVENTEEN

WHERE ARE YOU PERFORMING?

THERE ARE DIFFERENT types of performance required depending on where the performance is taking place. A TV performance should be totally different from a live performance to 10,000 people, which in turn should be different from an intimate club gig. They key question should always be, 'How do I engage my audience?'

Audition panel – This has to be one of the toughest situations to perform in. A handful of tough-looking people behind a table are very intimidating. The best advice we can give you is to keep your performance comfortable and allow your inner confidence to shine through. If you are cockily confident (surface confidence) it puts people off and, equally, if you are shy it makes the panel feel awkward. Don't try to be something you are not. If you win their approval by pretending to be somebody else you will then spend the rest of your career trying to convince them of who you really are. Be authentic.

DAVID: When we were auditioning the final ninety for *Fame Academy* we gave each person a couple of tries at their song. When we were down to the final forty-five we gave each person a full fifteen minutes. We understand how nervous people are at auditions. You don't always see them at their best so if you try to make the audition space a little more like a rehearsal space it's amazing how much more an artist will give you.

Showcase – A showcase is a small gig that is put on for a select group of people. For example, if a record company are interested in signing you they will probably ask to see a performance. These performances sometimes take place at the record company itself or in a high quality rehearsal studio. They also take place when a record company wants to show TV executives their new act for possible television appearances. They have a similar feel to an audition because a record company audience tends not to react very much. They play it cool. Don't be intimidated. They might love it but they won't necessarily show it!

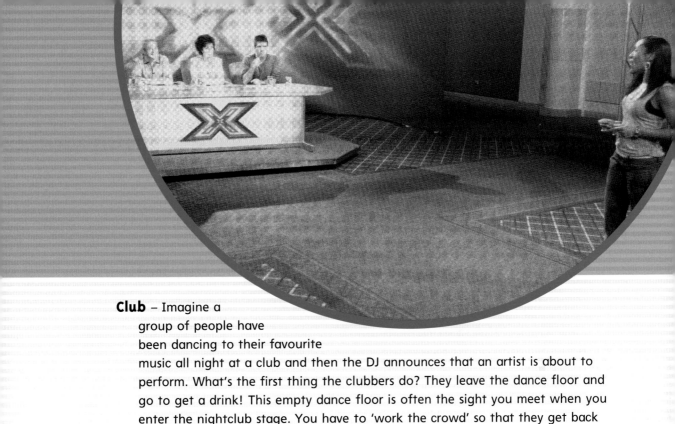

Club – Imagine a
group of people have
been dancing to their favourite
music all night at a club and then the DJ announces that an artist is about to
perform. What's the first thing the clubbers do? They leave the dance floor and
go to get a drink! This empty dance floor is often the sight you meet when you
enter the nightclub stage. You have to 'work the crowd' so that they get back
on the dance floor. Check out the teaching on talking to your audience later in
this chapter.

Pub – The thing to remember when you perform in most pub situations is that
the audience is usually there for two things: to drink and to chat. This forms
a barrier between you and your audience and you must have the confidence
to break through it. How much you intrude and demand their attention
has to be kept in a fine balance. We recommend you absolutely enjoy your
own performance and if they begin to look like they are too then take the
opportunity to chat.

Theatre – The lights in a theatre are usually very bright so you will not be able
to see much beyond the first few rows of seats. Don't be fooled – you have
many rows behind these and often up higher too so don't forget to play to
the whole theatre. If you want to break into musical theatre it is not enough
just to be a good singer. You must have other skills alongside this. The three
musical theatre disciplines are singing, dancing and acting. You must be able
to perform to a high standard in any two of the three and be competent at
the third. Your strongest skill will dictate the type of work you get. Many
people we meet are in West End shows and many are dissatisfied with the
roles they are being given. The most common reason for them not gaining the

roles they desire is that their acting is not strong enough so they always end up in the chorus or in smaller roles. A friend of ours was playing good singing and dancing roles   in many West End shows but wanted to be seen for more dramatic roles. She gave up her West End work to go back and study and as a result has gone on to play dramatic roles. Of course much can and is learned along the way but it's probably best to hone as many skills as you can before embarking on the journey.

Arenas and larger venues – It's tempting to play to the front section of the audience when you are in a bigger venue. As with a theatre, the lights do not allow you to see to the people at the back. Break up the audience into three specific areas: left side, middle and right side. Mark out in your set at what point you will play each side area. Also, remember your face is often twelve feet high on two screens either side of the stage, so watch out for your facial expressions. Because of the screens your performance can be both big and small. You can both order the audience about and be chatty with them. Ideally, they should feel the performance is both an en masse and intimate experience.

TV – If you are performing on TV the size of performance has to be small. The camera is the vehicle that takes you to the audience who are sitting on sofas up and down the country, not dancing in the aisles of a stadium. It doesn't mean you shouldn't move but be aware that if the director has asked for a close up of your face and you are busy bobbing up and down it will look strange! You can always ask someone if you can have a look at the camera script. Even though the director may change a few shots on the recording, it will give you a rough idea of the parts of the song when you are on a close up, a mid-shot or a full-length shot. Some people feel camera shy when they first have to perform on TV. Remember, it's only a black box. When you arrive at the studio don't be afraid to have a good look down the lens and as we mentioned in chapter three, own your space – including the cameras.

It is always interesting to watch the performers on big televised events. Generally, the younger artists perform for the crowds in front of them live on TV around the globe. In contrast, the older, more experienced artists are so much more aware that their target audience was the home viewer. We would say the priority audience in this case is the TV audience. Whether it's a handful of people or thousands, don't get swept away by those in front of you during televised performances.

Whatever the environment you are performing in, remember you have the authority and you are in control of the space. If you read what look like apathetic expressions on the audience's faces try not to react. If you continue in confidence they will eventually join you! It's a bit like driving a car: if you prove you are a trustworthy driver people will not be afraid to jump on board. If you show a lack of self-belief they will not get behind you.

PERFORMANCE SPACE

When you watch a performance you can always tell the size of the space a singer has rehearsed in. If they have been confined to a tiny rehearsal studio they will normally only cover the space on stage that they have been used to performing in. Equally, if they are used to a bigger space and are now confined to a postage stamp-sized stage they will stomp around with a physically huge performance.

When preparing for a big tour most bands go through three stages of rehearsal space. They will start in a small environment, even a dance studio if they are a non-instremental band. From there they will go to a larger studio where they will have a small raised stage area and the musicians will be set on to this stage. Finally they will go into what's called production rehearsals, where the stage they will be touring with will be set up exactly as it will be when the tour begins.

Try to adapt to the size of stage you are performing on, especially if you have dance routines as well. If you are moving to a larger stage work out the space when you arrive at the venue. If you are working on a smaller stage then you have ample opportunity when you are in your rehearsal space to mark out the stage dimensions with tape and try to stay within them.

TALKING

Talking to the audience can be the most intimidating part of a set for some artists. They are confident in the music, the song-singing and the moves but the idea of having to say something can be terrifying. This is probably because, compared to the amount of rehearsal that goes into the other areas, the talking part is often left until the artist is on stage. It's an after thought. The main thing to remember is that the audience will normally do what you tell them to do. If you believe you have total authority and speak out of that authority then chances are the audience will do as you say. If you tell them to throw their arms in the air, they will. If you gingerly give them the option to throw their arms in the air they probably won't. There is nothing wrong with having a few remarks worked out. Experience will make you more spontaneous and relaxed. Take time to work out your style.

CHAPTER EIGHTEEN

WHAT TYPE OF SINGING VOICE DO YOU HAVE?

VOCAL TYPES

There are lots of different types of singers and all have their strengths and weaknesses. Listening to singers talk about their voices can be similar to listening to people talk about their hair. Those who have curly hair want straight hair and those with straight hair want it to be curly! Try to be excited and passionate about what you have and appreciate how much you can grow within your particular style or type of singing.

Tonal – Tonal singers are those whose voices have a great sound. It is not so much about what they can do with the voice but more about the quality and tone of the sound they produce. The voice will have a resonance and presence that moves the listener.

Dynamic – Dynamic singers will not necessarily have a great tonal quality to their voices but it is what they are able to do with their voices that makes them great. Their range, control and ability to go where they want, when they want, moves the listener.

Emotional – If you have neither a tonal nor dynamic voice don't worry, you may still be able to sell a song. Singers who are able to convey emotions in a powerful way are great. They will be able to communicate anger, fear, love and the whole gamut of emotions in order to move their listeners.

Many singers have the most technically correct voices and yet lack any kind of identity. They may be great at imitating the singers they love to listen to but have no sense of their own voice. Take the time to develop your sound.

When you are listening to your voice mentally earmark the things you think sound good or distinguishable and then (keeping your technique) feature them in your performance.

Listening to music and taking note of how others do it can be very helpful. You don't have to sound the same but you can pick up some of the tricks! There are many ways to sell a song so try not to compare yourself too much with other singers.

PERFORMANCE TYPES

All relationships work best when there is good communication. When you perform for an audience you enter into a relationship with them. What do you want your relationship to be like? What do you want to communicate?

You may find the following types helpful when looking at different reasons for, and styles of, communication. These examples are not hard and fast – you may be a combination of all of them. Neither are they the only facets of performance communication. Music and the arts are capable of expressing just about every emotion known to humanity. These are here to help you to start thinking as a communicator.

I am an 'Entertainer' – You use your performance purely to entertain. You want your audience to go away feeling fantastic. You understand that your audience may have had a bad day or be feeling low and it's your job to take them on a journey to where they can forget about the other parts of their lives and enjoy the music. Your audience may need to escape from their own reality. How do you help them to do this through your performance and communication and how do you maintain the feel-good factor throughout?

Artists who would have 'Entertainer' as their primary form of communication would be Robbie Williams, Lady Gaga, Tina Turner, Rhianna and Beyonce.

I am a 'Challenger' – You use your performance to ask questions, to make people think. You want your audience to go away questioning their previous worldview and challenged by yours. You may be political or simply analytical. You are not afraid to shake your audience out of their comfort zone. You are a peacemaker not a peacekeeper. You aren't prepared to keep the peace – as a peacemaker you will undo in order to make right. You are not afraid to show anger – anger can be good when it is not destructive. You make or sing music for the brain as well as the feet!

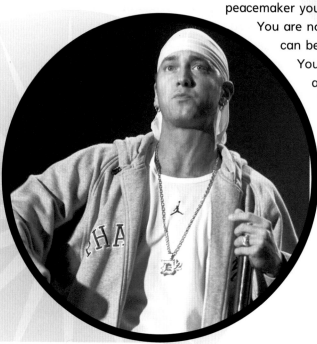

Artists who would have 'Challenger' as their primary form of communication would be Jay Z, Eminem, Curtis Mayfield, U2 and Billy Bragg.

I am an 'Inspirer' – You use your performance to give hope, to make people feel that they can be what they want to be. Your music may have lots of personal testimony. You are not afraid to show the dark side of life. Only when darkness is seen to be totally dark can we really appreciate how truly amazing the light is. If your lyrics tell of the brilliant things that have happened in your life they will be made all the more brilliant when you show how much it cost you and how hard you had to struggle to get to where you are. Your music will communicate frailty in order to show strength and this will inspire your audience.

Artists who would have 'Inspirer' as their primary form of communication would be Annie Lennox, Mary J Blige, Mumford & Sons and Bob Marley.

I am a 'Mover' – You use your performance to make people face their emotions. You love to bring a 'tingle factor' to your performance. You take your audience on a journey through sadness, joy, laughter, anger, love and all stops in between. You may do this through lyrics or you may do it simply through your physical or vocal communication. You are the torch singer, the one who people hold their lighters up to!

Artists who would have 'Mover' as their primary form of communication would be Leona Lewis, Luther Vandross, Celine Dion and Adele.

INTROVERT VS EXTROVERT

As you can see from the previous page, there are different types of performers using their skills to say what they want. On another note there are different performance styles too. This goes back to the relationship factor. Are you an introvert or an extrovert performer? The definition of introvert is 'someone who gains energy from being on their own'. The definition of extrovert is 'someone who gains energy from being around others'. These definitions help us as we come to look at introvert and extrovert performers.

Introvert – The introvert performer's attitude on stage is that they perform in their own world while the audience views them. The artist enjoys his or her own voice and performance and as the audience observes the artist's enjoyment they enter the artist's world. These artists always keep a healthy emotional distance from the audience.

Extrovert – The extrovert performer's attitude on stage is that they want to join with their audience, lead them on a journey, taking them through a completely shared experience. The artist will often feel very comfortable chatting to the audience or giving them directions that help them to take part in the overall performance. They are united with their audience and have a 'we' mentality.

You may find that your performance changes from one to the other at different stages in your life depending on what you feel comfortable with and what is desired from your communication.

CHOOSING THE RIGHT SONG FOR YOUR VOICE

If you do not sing your own material it's important to choose the right songs for your voice. For instance, we hear many singers with gentle voices trying to sing the hugely powered vocals of a Mariah Carey or Whitney Houston song. It's more impressive if you sing something within your vocal ability. Remember that we have all heard great singers sing these classics so unless you are going to interpret the song in a totally different way you have to be able at least to match or better the original performance. If you can't, then stay away from those songs. Try to choose songs that show your vocal strengths, not your vocal weaknesses.

Equally, choose a lyric that is believable coming from you. That is not to say you can only sing lyrics you have experienced but hearing a 16-year-old sing a song about getting divorced and getting used to being alone is not believable.

A question we are often asked is: 'Is it bad for me to sing other artist's songs?' Our answer is yes and no. If you listen to other great singers it can be good for developing different tones. What you should avoid is copying the whole performance. It's great to be able to say, 'I sound like Rhianna', but Rhianna sounds like Rhianna, that's her identity. No record company is going to want a copycat artist. You must find your own sound. Sounding identical also makes you come across like a karaoke singer, which is great if that's what you want to do but not so good if you want to make a career in the music industry.

YES BUT: My voice seems to be changing constantly so I can't tell what type of singer I am.

ANSWER: The voice changes constantly throughout life. It evolves and grows and as we explore it more of it gets unlocked. However, the type of singer you are will normally be dictated by 'who' you are, your worldview and your personality.

CHAPTER NINETEEN

KNOWING YOUR VOCAL ROOTS

LEARNING THE ORIGINS

This chapter seeks to give you a rough potted history of some of the most popular singers involved in the evolution of different genres of music.

Knowing the roots of your vocal style can be really helpful when it comes to exploring your own identity. Many singers never look beyond the stars of the day. By taking a look at what came before we often find some real nuggets of information that can help us to develop the voice. These few examples are here to give you a taster in order to encourage you to explore further the roots of the particular styles you enjoy and might want to sing. You may find you love many different styles – that's OK too.

VOCAL IDENTITY

Male soul – If you like Usher, Ne-Yo, Pharrell Williams, Taio Cruz, Cee Lo Green and Chris Brown, check out Stevie Wonder, Marvin Gaye and Curtis Mayfield. Back in the 1960s the great solo singers were people like Otis Redding, Sam Cook, James Brown and Wilson Pickett. They influenced artists like Marvin Gaye, Al Green and Donny Hathaway. Donny Hathaway's vocal style, in particular, influenced Stevie Wonder who, in turn, influenced a whole generation of R'n'B singers. More recently singers have been reaching back for the smooth 70's soul sounds of Marvin Gaye, Al Green and Ted Pendergrass.

Female soul – If you like Alicia Keyes, Beyonce, Rhianna, Leona Lewis and Jesse J., then have a listen to Dionne Warwick, Aretha Franklin, The Emotions, Roberta Flack, Gladys Knight, Diana Ross and Patti La Belle. The wonderful thing about these early singers was their vocal identity. They had real soul and were not afraid to show emotion. They didn't riff too heavily; they let their vocal tone and the emotion of the lyric sell the song.

It was great working with Roberta Flack and Diana Ross. They are both such different singers but both equally in control of their voices. Diana Ross rarely riffs and sings with hardly any volume and yet the dynamics and drama of her voice are so distinctive and soulful.

Rock – If you love Radiohead, Coldplay and Elbow, check out The Beatles, Pink Floyd and U2. When The Beatles began Paul McCartney said, 'We started off by imitating Elvis, Chuck Berry, Carl Perkins, Gene Vincent, The Coasters, The Drifters – we just copied what they did'. Many artists find their identity by being an amalgam of everything they like and admire.

Pop – If you are a Justin Beiber, Justin Timberlake, Lady Gaga, Mylee Cyrus or Katy Perry fan check out Michael Jackson, Madonna or Hall & Oates. For instance, Justin Timberlake's use of his falsetto voice is almost identical to Michael Jackson's early music, particularly the *Off The Wall* album.

Pop/rock – If you are a Kaiser Chiefs, The Script, Pink, or Florence and the Machine admirer, check out The Who, Tina Turner, The Small Faces, Elton John, Sham 69 and REM. You can hear some of the drama and grandeur of 70's Elton John in Robbie's music.

Indie – If you love Arctic Monkeys, The Strokes and Razorlight, then check out David Bowie, The Cure and Suede. Back in the 1960s the actor/singer Anthony Newly had a few big hits using a very distinctive London accent. Soon after, David Bowie did the same on his first recordings and created a whole new sound. With indie music it's not about perfect tuning. The voice is often used in a more spoken way and the vowels are normally severely distorted.

Country – If you like Taylor Swift, and Carrie Underwood, check out Tammy Wynette, Dolly Parton, Reba McEntire and Garth Brookes. Country singers are very narrative and if you listen to the current artists they are breaking new ground, introducing Country to Pop music in the same way as those earlier artists did in their eras.

Jazz – If you like Amy Winehouse, Michael Buble or Nora Jones, you'll probably love Sarah Vaughn, Ella Fitzgerald and Frank Sinatra. Harry Connick Junior's phrasing and timing are heavily influenced by Sinatra.

Rap – If you're a Jay Z, 50 Cent, Eminem, Nicky Minage or Tinie Tempah fan, you should check out Ice T, MC Search, Queen Latifa and Coolio. The important thing with rap is that the tone of voice, the timing and the way you phrase has to be distinctive and identifiable. Many people think that rap is just a bit of talking over a rhythm but if you study good rappers their rhymes are very clever and each artist has their own sound.

So are we saying that all these modern artists are merely imitators? Far from it. Musical originality usually comes from a talented person or people fusing all the things that influence them, filtering them through their own imagination and creativity to come up with something unique. This in turn becomes the catalyst for creativity in the next generation.

It is also helpful to have a knowledge of who produces who. Quite often the same producer will be working on three or four of the top acts and it helps when in discussion about your music to have an idea about who is out there, who's hot and who is producing who.

As we said before, listening to music and taking note of how others do it can be very helpful. You don't have to sound the same but you can pick up some of their tricks and, with Sir Paul McCartney's attitude, become an amalgamation of everything you admire!

YES BUT: I want to do my thing, not sound like others, right? So why do I need to look at older, past artists.

ANSWER: Absolutely you should be doing your own thing. The idea is you learn and understand your history. It should inform, not dictate, your music.

CHAPTER TWENTY

GROUP AND BACKING VOCALS

IT ALWAYS AMAZES US when singers think of backing vocals as the job they will do if they don't make it as – or aren't quite good enough to be – lead vocalists. A truly professional backing vocalist (or session singer) will be an amazing singer, have the ability to do just about anything with their voice and will normally have more musical discipline that a lead vocalist. It is also a very difficult business to break into.

There are a few things you will need if you are going to be a good session singer.

Blending – The whole idea of backing vocals is that no one voice stands out. The overall effect should be that of a wall of sound against which the lead vocal can stand out. This is where being able to blend is so important. Blending is being able to make your voice sound the same as the other backing vocalists around you. This demands that you make your voice more like theirs and that they make their voice more like yours. This means that pronunciation, timing, tone and tuning all have to be mirrored among the group of backing singers.

DAVID: I remember a few years ago when Carrie and I were putting a section of twenty singers together for Diana Ross we automatically thought of choosing the most impressive lead vocalists available. But what was required were the best blenders, and these are not necessarily the best lead singers. Eventually, we opted for the people who would not be trying to stand out individually but be able to work as a team.

Slipstreaming – This is where one singer has the exact 'sound' required for the track and the other singer(s) back up this singer by reinforcing the sound. If the main backing vocal (BV) singer is standing straight on to the microphone the slipstreaming person will stand behind their shoulder and literally copy

exactly what they do. We sometimes call these main BV singers 'pointers' because they point the way the sound should go.

CARRIE: I remember when I was first asked to sing backing vocals I learned so much from slipstreaming David. Hearing how he did things and then copying him, standing over his shoulder, fattening or brightening up his sound made a great blend and we soon found ourselves working constantly.

Listening – This is absolutely fundamental to backing vocals. The ability to hear exactly what it is the producer requires and then listening to the rest of the team to make sure you deliver the producer's brief takes skill.

We mentioned earlier about pronunciation, timing and tonal quality so let's take a look at these. Obviously, if you read music this is good as most of the timings and certainly all the notes will be there, but what a sheet of music cannot explain is pronunciation, tone and the general vibe and feel of a track.

Pronunciation – You have to make sure every word is pronounced in exactly the same way with the same vowel sounds, crescendos and speeds of vibrato, etc. For instance, if you have too many people pronouncing the letter 'S' or 'T' in a lyric then it may be worth appointing one person to sing these and have everyone else sing them silently.

Timing – It is essential that all timing is identical. The way a lyric bounces and moves along must be mirrored by all the backing vocalists. The ends of lines should have the same number of beats. Is the line coming off after four, five or six beats? Are you holding it for eight or coming off on eight? These are all things that need to be discussed. Sometimes singers have a tendency to rush ahead of the beat. Try to stay on the beat or, for a funkier feel, marginally behind the beat.

Tone – Probably the most telling aspect of a good BV section is their ability to make all the voices sound the same tonally. Is the sound required airy, warm, full, breathy, gentle, shouty, insistent, regal, triumphant, joyous, hollow, sad or angry? There are so many things to be heard in the tone of a voice.

Harmonies – If you are someone who freezes at the thought of having to learn a harmony don't worry, you are not alone. Many people who are great lead vocalists have real fears about being able to sing in harmony. If you struggle with harmonies try to think of the part you are asked to sing as the melody. Put all other notes out of your head and bulldoze your note through. Once you've got it then start to listen to the other harmonies and blend your voice with the other singers.

Counterpart – Counterpart or counter melody is where you have two different melody lines going on at the same time, sometimes with different lyrics or sounds ('OOH' and 'AAH', etc).

Choir – A choir sound can be slightly looser in terms of the blend as there are more voices being used. Be aware of tuning. Because the vocals are often loud one person may go out of tune. Before you know it a few others have followed and then the whole section starts to sound badly out of tune. Having said this, there is nothing like the passionate sound of many voices singing together.

Tracking up – When you record in the studio you will often be asked to track up your vocals. This means you will record a particular part a few times over to build up the sound. If you are singing in a group you may all sing different harmonies and all be recorded at the same time. Equally, you could all learn and sing each single harmony through together so that the producer can have more control over each harmony. Sometimes you will record a part quietly the first time and the second time more forcefully so that the overall sound has both power and fullness.

Recording – Some producers like to have one microphone with everyone situated around it. Others like to have a separate mic for each harmony, so there would usually be three mics in a line. Still others use overhead mics to pick up the ambient sound (overall sound at a distance), particularly if there are large numbers of singers. Some use a combination of mics to give both a close and an ambient sound.

DISCIPLINE

One of the hardest things to do when learning a new song is to learn your part when there are other people singing a different part loudly next to you. Whoever is leading the session will expect you to be listening during the teaching period. A strange thing that many of the singers we have worked with do is to sing along the minute you start teaching them. How can you listen properly if you are already singing? The reason singers do this is because they are afraid they may not get the notes quickly enough and they are afraid the leader of the session may move on to the next part before they have learned theirs. Don't panic! Most good session leaders or arrangers will take you through your part a few times. Take a couple of goes just to listen to the part before you even attempt to join in. Once the session leader has given you your part and it is learnt, try to remain silent while other parts are being taught.

LEAD VOCALS

When we produce vocals for a solo artist very often we will use backing vocalists for the BV parts even if the artist is capable of singing the BV parts. We do this because we want the lead vocal to sit on top of the BVs and stand out. When a singer does their own BVs there is a danger they will end up blending with themselves and the individual sound can be lost.

YES BUT: I can't do harmonies. I just can't get them.

ANSWER: For some people learning harmonies comes naturally. For others it's a skill that needs to be learned. It's partly ear training and learning to listen properly, but mostly it's confidence that needs to be grown. If you think you won't get the harmony, you're probably right. If you believe you can, then you probably will!

CHAPTER TWENTY-ONE

TECHIE STUFF

SOUND CHECKING

One of the most daunting things a singer has to do is to check the sound for a live performance. We have seen singers who are seasoned professionals almost crumble at the thought of having to communicate with a sound engineer. It is probably because artists think there is a huge divide between themselves and the technical people – they speak a different language!

Sound checking is a skill that can be learned and one that most artists never get the opportunity to master because rarely does anyone take the time to teach them how to do it. They're normally expected to fumble through.

If the sound isn't coming back at you the way you want to hear it that's probably because, together with your sound person, you haven't worked it out yet. Not being able to hear yourself is different from not liking or not being used to the sound you are hearing. A sound check is not the place to have a crisis of confidence even if you are not hearing what you want to hear. Getting used to hearing yourself, whether live or in the studio, takes time but after a while you'll get used to hearing your voice in a new way.

It's often good, when sound checking for a live performance, to know the names of a few pieces of equipment and to have an understanding of what they do.

On-stage monitors – In front of you will be one or more speakers called 'on-stage monitors' (which are sometimes called 'wedges' because of the way they are shaped). These are there to provide a sound mix purely for you and normally you will be able to ask the sound engineer to take the keyboard – or any other instrument – up or down in volume in the monitors until you are happy with the balance between the instrumentation and yourself. Each member of the band will have these monitors too, although sometimes they have to be shared.

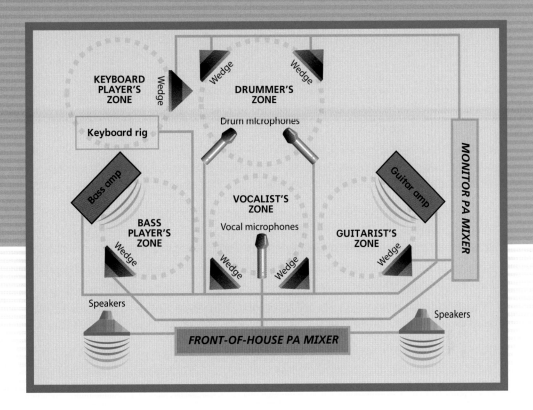

Front-of-house speakers – These are the speakers that feed the sound to the audience.

Mixing desk – This is the desk that the sound engineer sits behind. It has things called faders on it. These are the rows of buttons that the engineer slides up and down, controlling the volume of each instrument and voice. The rows themselves are known as channels and if there are enough of them it means each instrument can have its own channel. If there are fewer channels then the musicians on stage will have to share the same sound mix. For instance, the lead singer may have the same sound in his or her monitors as the backing vocalists.

On-stage sound engineer – At bigger concerts you will have you own on-stage sound engineer. They deal with on-stage monitoring only and so they are your best friend! He or she is the person whose job it is to make sure you have the sound you need in your monitors to make your performance work.

Front-of-house sound engineer – This is the person who makes sure the sound is good for the audience. If you have a separate on-stage sound engineer they will only deal with the front-of-house monitoring.

What to do? – We find it best to sound check for a live performance initially with the front-of-house speakers turned off. This allows you to get a good idea of what you will be hearing on the night. We are continually amazed, when you have the front-of-house engineers doing all the sound, at just how many don't even realise the on-stage monitors are not turned on. If you get them to turn the front-of-house monitors off it immediately shows if you have any on-stage sound at all. From where you stand on stage the bodies in the audience will swallow up most of the front-of-house sound so the monitors in front of you on the stage should you give you everything you need.

It's best to sing a part of one of the songs you are going to perform without any accompaniment. Try to choose a song that takes in the quieter and the louder parts of your voice. Always sound check at the same volume you will be singing at during the performance. Hold your mic right up to your mouth and don't pull it away when you sing louder – any good sound engineer will ride the faders on the mixing desk! (In plain English that means that they will push the buttons up on the mixer if you sing too quietly and down if you sing too loudly.)

Bottom – If your voice sounds dull and dreary compared to how you are used to hearing it the mic probably has what we call 'too much bottom' on it and you will need to ask the sound engineer if they can 'roll some of the bottom off'.

Toppy – If your voice sounds thin and tinny compared to how you are used to hearing it the mic probably has what's known as 'too much top' on it or it is not bassy enough. You need to ask the sound engineer if they can 'roll some of the top off or add some bass'.

Boxy – Sometimes the mic sound will be 'boxy', giving the impression that your voice is trapped in a box. This normally means that there is too much mid in the sound, particularly the lower mid. Tell them it's 'a bit boxy' and they should sort it out.

Gain – If your sound engineer comments that they don't have enough gain on the mic this basically means that you are not giving them enough volume to work with. You will need to sing louder or hold the mic closer to your mouth.

Dbs – The full name for these is 'decibels'. These are the units that sound is measured in. The louder the sound the more Dbs there will be, and vice versa.

Signal – This is another name for the sound level.

Feedback – This is normally caused by the engineer turning you up too loud. Be aware though that they may have done so because you are not giving them enough volume or have said you cannot hear enough of yourself. Feedback can also be caused by the singer turning the top of the microphone toward the on-stage monitors. Try always to keep the mic facing you.

Once you are happy with your voice through the monitors it's time to add the backing vocals and sounds from the musicians. You can ask for more piano, less guitar and so on and, providing you are not sharing the same sound channel as the backing vocals, you will be able to ask for them to be higher, lower or taken away completely. If you have keyboards being played in your band it may be helpful to have them higher in your mix as they will help you to stay in tune.

If you start a song don't wait to the end to tell the engineer what you want. This is a sound check not a rehearsal so stops and starts are OK. Once you have run a song and feel happy then ask the engineer to put the front-of-house sound back in.

In-ears – These are the tiny earpieces you wear to hear your sound directly in your ears instead of hearing it through the monitors. They are like personal stereo headphones but moulded into the shell shape of your ear. They are basically a tiny version of your on-stage monitors but the sound will be closer to you as they are literally in your ears. They take a bit of getting used to but most live artists today wear them. You will also have to wear a belt with what's known as a 'pack', which picks up the signal for the in-ears so that they work. The pack has its own volume control so you can turn the overall volume up or down manually. If you have in-ears fitted make sure you do not wear one in and one out. This can cause deafness as you tend to ask for the one that is left in your ear to be turned up too loud.

You will have noticed that some singers stick one finger into their ear when they are performing live. This is when they are working with monitors and they need to check they are in tune and are not sure of the sound. This is OK to do for odd moments but by listening to the sound in your ear you stop listening to the music and therefore you could be perfectly in tune with yourself and yet totally out of tune with the overall sound. We think it looks bad if you do it all the time, if your sound is good you shouldn't need to do it at all.

MICROPHONES FOR LIVE WORK

Microphones come in all sorts of different shapes and sizes and have many different uses depending on the situation. It's important to learn how to hold your mic. Most mics for live singing are what we call 'directional', which means the sound works best when you are singing directly down the mic. The closer you are to the mic the bassier and fuller the sound quality will be and the further away you are the thinner it will sound. This is known as the 'proximity effect'.

Do not hold the mic down, like a lolly

Do not cup the mic

Do hold the mic up

Lead mic – This is a hand-held mic with a long lead attached to it.

Radio mic – This is a hand-held mic that has no lead.

Head mic - This is a mic worn on the head. In our experience the sound quality doesn't seem to be as good as a straightforward hand-held mic.

Lapel mic – You may need to wear one of these if you are being interviewed on TV or sometimes when working in the theatre. Also known as a clip mic or tie mic, this is the mic that is clipped to the front of your clothes or – for the theatre – sometimes rests in your hair. You will have to wear a battery pack on a belt or clipped to your waistband. This picks up the signal so the mic works.

MICROPHONES FOR THE STUDIO

Microphones for recording sessions are normally quite different from the ones you would use in a live situation. You can often sing all the way round the mic as they have a multi-directional function (omni). Some producers and singers like to use valve mics. These use a valve system in the inner workings of the mic. This can make the voice sound warmer and fuller, depending on the singer. Ribbon mics also work well, giving the singer a smoother sound.

Different mics work well for different singers. Once a singer arrives at the sound they like they tend to use it the whole time.

MIC STANDS

When you are singing live there are a few different types of mic stand you may choose or be given. See the pictures below.

Hydraulic – Some mic stands move up and down with hydraulic movement. You squeeze the bar in the middle of the mic stand to move it up or down.

VOCAL SOUND EFFECTS

Sound effects can make a huge difference to the voice and it's important to work out the effects that make your voice come alive when recorded or singing live. They can add fullness and resonance to the voice, but it's always worth remembering that the sound engineer can only work with the voice he or she is given. Improvement is possible, miracles take a little longer!

Reverb – This is literally 'reverberation', an effect which makes the voice sound fuller.

Echo – Also known as 'delay', this is a repeat of the voice coming after the original source.

Compression – This is where the dynamics of the voice are squeezed closer together so that the loud parts of the voice are not too loud and the quiet parts not too quiet.

Cans – This is another word for the headphones you wear when you are recording in the studio. For better tuning, professionals wear one can off and one on.

Pop shield – Pop shields come in two formats, the first is the more obvious foam cover that fits neatly over the mic. The second is a shield made of nylon tights-type fabric which stands between the singer and the microphone in the recording studio. Sometimes thrown together from a bent coat hanger and a stocking, pop shields help to mask any sibilance in the voice or 'popping' on percussive sounds, such as 'P's and 'B's.

YES BUT: I can be great at home, but the minute I sing on mic I hate the sound and I start to lose confidence.

ANSWER: We have seen so many people melt down when they come to sound check. It's because they have singing skills and yet no language to communicate with a soundperson. You have to learn the language and say to yourself, 'It's not that I'm a bad singer it's just that we haven't got the sound right yet.' Be patient.

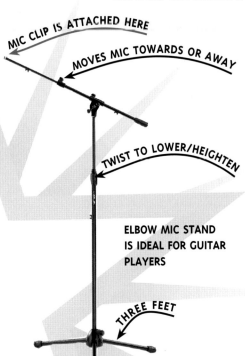

MIC CLIP IS ATTACHED HERE

MOVES MIC TOWARDS OR AWAY

TWIST TO LOWER/HEIGHTEN

ELBOW MIC STAND IS IDEAL FOR GUITAR PLAYERS

THREE FEET

HYDRAULIC ACTION MOVES STAND HIGHER/LOWER

MIC CLIP IS ATTACHED HERE

CIRCULAR BASE MIC STAND IS GREAT IF YOU WANT TO PULL STAND TOWARDS YOU

trusting relationship with honest and encouraging people they will thrive. We totally believe in how good the artist can be at the same time as being fully aware of how good they currently are. In our communication we try to inspire the artist toward what they can be while showing them how to be aware of their current weaknesses.

Critique points out the things that need to be changed. Change can be both exhilarating and frightening. Ask yourself the question: Do I see change as an opportunity or a threat? The minute an artist chooses not to listen to good advice they cease to grow. Coaching without critique is flattery and the student can never fully develop.

CRITIQUE

CARRIE: When I was asked to be a tutor/judge on BBC's *Fame Academy* I really wanted to make sure my analysis was as helpful and yet as honest as possible. I believe the audience at home understands a lot more than we credit them for. They may not be able to analyse why they don't enjoy a performance but they do know when there is something not quite right. Time after time, during the filming of the series, members of the public would approach me in the supermarket and chat about what I had said during the show the night before. Because they had heard a professional analyse the performance it gave them the language they needed to critique the performances themselves.

In normal life, when artists come off a stage they are always desperate to know if they have done well. They are normally glad if you tell them, for instance, that they need to look at verse two of a particular song. When it comes to reality TV that same critique is given in front of millions of viewers and it can be a lot harder to take!

PERSEVERENCE

A career in the arts is not for the faint-hearted but we are convinced that if you commit to improving and persevere then eventually you will get a break, no matter how small. The comedian Tommy Cooper had a great saying: 'If you stay in the business for long enough someone will employ you.' That is so encouraging and it's a saying we have held on to through some of the professionally harder times we've been through in the past couple of decades.

David: When I started to have hit records in the 1980s people assumed success had come from nowhere. I had a band called Linx and my partner and I found a manager but no one would give us a record deal. I had given up a career in journalism to be a nighttime security guard so I could spend my days in the recording studio. We spent our last savings on pressing up a hundred copies of our record and managed to get a copy into the hands of the DJ Robbie Vincent. Robbie played the record on his radio show on a Saturday and by the Monday we had three offers on the table. Only those close to us knew just how close we were to giving up and how broke we were. It took years to become an overnight success!

FORM AND FLOW

We sometimes train people from a variety of areas of business, from The Foreign and Commonwealth Commission to The Body Shop, from Sainsbury's to the District Audit Office! One of the areas we teach on is 'Form and Flow'. Most business groups work in either one mode or the other.

Form – This is where you decide your goals and exactly what path you are to take and then you set about accomplishing your plans stage by stage. The advantage of Form is that you plan and set out your goals. The disadvantage is that you will not be prepared to take up an opportunity that suddenly arises if it falls outside of your plans and you will not be able easily to re-form your plans should something unexpectedly go wrong.

Flow – This is where you wait to see what comes your way and then move with it. The advantage of Flow is that if opportunities arise you are always in a position to move with them and when great but unexpected opportunities occur you are willing to explore these new avenues. The disadvantage is that you have no set plans and could be wasting time sitting around waiting for a desirable opportunity to come along.

The ideal situation is to use the two methods together so you have plans but you are flexible enough to move with the opportunities that arise and are prepared to re-write the plans if things are flourishing in a different direction.

If someone had told us ten years ago we were going to be leading vocal coaches we would have laughed at them and inwardly felt disappointed. Our aim was always to be artists ourselves. When we look at what has happened to us it's truly amazing and vocal coaching has turned out to be the most fantastic job. We had our plans and yet were prepared to be flexible with them and in an unexpected way have fulfilled many of our dreams.

INNOVATION, IMPLEMENTATION AND REALISATION

These are three stages of career building that can help you to achieve your goals.

Innovation – This is all about dreaming big dreams. It's about brainstorming and coming up with great and original ideas. But these ideas mean nothing without implementation.

Implementation – This is the process of work needed to achieve end goals. It's about settling down to the hard graft of achieving your goals.

Realisation – This is the point at which you can stand back and admire your work and what you have managed to achieve; where you can see the fulfilment of dreams before you.

If you have good ideas but do not work out how to implement them they will only ever stay 'good ideas'. Equally, if you are great at admin, the process and all the 'doing' stuff but don't have original ideas then all your efforts will come to nothing.

Many artists are great with ideas but don't realise that a singing career demands time, effort and many mundane activities that have to be done in order to achieve goals. Implementation without realisation leaves you feeling a failure, even when you have achieved great things. Don't get so tied down in the doing that you neglect to appreciate what you have already done. So many artists have their number one album and then spend the whole time worrying about how to achieve the next goal. Success is a lot more enjoyable when you remember the price you've had to pay for it.

If you dream of it, work for it. If, having worked for it, you get it then enjoy it. When you have taken the time to enjoy it, begin to dream again!

Index

This is a Carlton Book

Published by Carlton Books Limited 2011
20 Mortimer Street
London W1T 3JW

Text copyright © Carrie Grant and David Grant
(trading as 'In Voice') 2003, 2011
Design copyright © Carlton Books Limited 2003, 2011

A CIP catalogue record for this book is available
from the British Library.

ISBN 978 1 84732 415 3

CHAPTER TWENTY-TWO

ARE YOU READY FOR LIFT OFF?

FACING REJECTION

Performing for an audience is the first step. The next step is convincing the bosses, TV and radio and the press. Welcome to the 'lion's den'! It's the hard but necessary step you have to take if you want to have a career involving singing, and it doesn't stop when you get a record deal. You will always face the possibility of rejection. Radio has to love your record, TV has to love your record and the public have to love your record. What about the press? What about when it comes to the follow-up record? What happens when another artist emerges in the same market as you and they now ride the crest of the wave? The potential for rejection never goes away, so the sooner you learn to live with it and deal with it the better. We know that sounds hard and we also know that in some ways it's almost impossible to do. It isn't easy, but knowing what is of real value, what really matters in your life, will help you to face each giant.

Try to put each knock-back into perspective. You are alive; you probably have someone who loves you; you probably have a roof over your head. Don't allow your career to take everything away from you. Remember the difference between rejection and critique. Many people confuse the two and often society demands that we only say good stuff even if it isn't true. We are in danger of nurturing an artistic community full of sycophants.

The music industry is full of hangers-on and sycophants. They survive in the industry because the artists need them to feed off. Their egos are satisfied with the fake and the false. We would say that one of the main reasons we work as vocal coaches to the extent we do is because we are both absolutely encouraging and at the same time absolutely honest. If an artist enters into a